True From

Seaward

Reminiscences of an old sea captain

by Captain Bill Sturrock

FIRST EDITION

Lorne Sailing School Brochure

Acknowledgements & Thanks

Sue Anderson
Photography and Art Design
Isle of Coll.

Lighthouse photographs courtesy of
Calum MacAulay

The Northern Lighthouse Board for allowing the
reproduction of sketches and plans.

Others as shown.

Cover from a painting by R. A. MacLeod

Sincere thanks to Ellen for patience and perseverance
beyond the call of duty in typing Bill's manuscripts.

Development editor Liam MacClarich

Contents

About the Author

Bill, born 1927

And the wheel's kick and the wind's song and the white sail's shaking,
And a grey mist on the sea's face, and a grey dawn breaking.

(John Masefield)

For some, the lure of the sea is irresistible. During WWII, sixteen-year-old Bill Sturrock left his home by the Tay Estuary to join the Blue Funnel Line. Before acceptance, he had to pass an Outward Bound course at Aberdovey.

This school was opened by Kurt Hahn, based on the same principles as Gordonston and what later became known as The Duke of Edinburgh Awards. The design aimed: "to give young seamen the ability to survive harsh conditions at sea by teaching confidence, tenacity, perseverance and to build experience of harsh conditions." An important element involved community service, especially in sea and mountain rescues.

Suitably toughened, Bill soon found himself at Matadi, ninety miles up the mighty River Congo.

Seafaring runs in his blood, and learning that he descends from the sister of the famous discoverer of Australia, Captain Cook, comes as no surprise.

Voyages round the world followed, as the young apprentice climbed the ranks. Reaching second mate, he joined the Royal

Mail Line and sailed to the West Indies. His duties included training many cadets.

Keen to get his first mate's ticket, he attended Dundee technical College. Fate intervened in the shape of American pilot officer John P. Noble. This airman loved danger and adventure. He had bought *Oregon*, a thirty-three foot yacht, and planned to sail from Tayport – on the East Coast of Scotland – across the Atlantic to America. Bill signed on as navigator.

After this memorable voyage, he joined the Blue Star Line and ran refrigerated cargoes from the River Plate in South America on the *Agentina Star*. Promotion soon followed to chief officer on the *Trojan Star*.

Argentina Star and Trojan Star

Family commitments led him to swallow the anchor in 1955. After a spell as assistant manager with Valentines of Dundee, he bought a hardware business in Tayport. This involved the responsibilities of printer, stationer, ironmonger, and gun-and-fishing-tackle merchant.

In 1968 he bought *Stormalong*, a twenty-eight-foot Falmouth Quay Punt (built in 1912), and sailed her for more than ten years during family holidays. A spell with the Royal Yachting Association as a Yachtmaster Instructor followed. A new challenge came in the form of a Colvic 29-6 hull and deck, for home completion. Bill worked on her himself then sailed to the West Coast. He skippered her as a sailing-school boat until 1983, when he replaced her with a 35-0 Jeanneau Melody. In seven years it logged more than 35,000 nautical miles.

Bill's daughter Wendy Christens Colvic Stormalong 2

In the winter of 1985/86, he had a *Para Handy* spell as skipper of the 370 ton Coaster *Eilan Rosin Dubh* plying between the Mersey and Stornoway. Various delivery trips from Ireland and Norway to Oban broke the routine.

Next, came qualification as yachtmaster examiner. In the early 1990s, he ran three-week trips to Iceland and the Faeroes.

Bill is always ready to assist a fellow mariner. On one memorable occasion while moored at Eigg, a well-spoken yachtmaster asked for some engineering help. His generator fan belt had snapped. Bill replied, "Pinch a pair of your wife's tights and tie them round the pulley wheels."

His weather-beaten face developed a pinker tinge when an acquaintance later told him that the yachtmaster was Commander Tim Laurence – Princess Ann's husband.

He has spent many happy hours modifying and repairing boats, and looked after a small fleet of yachts at Dunstaffnage Marina. A jack-of-all-trades, Bill still found time for shooting, fishing and writing for yachting magazines.

In his late eighties, this old seadog is still active, growing vegetables, flowers and fruit. He lives with his wife Ellen, and has two sons and two daughters.

The Boat That Bill Built "Dressed Overall"

THE BOMBAY BLAST

Before I had made up my mind about a career, I was given a wonderful book called "Ships And Men" by Shalimar, i.e., F. C.Henry. However, in the summer holidays, I convinced my dear mum that I wanted to go to sea in my older brother Forbes's footsteps. I think she was quite happy about that. So she organized an interview for me in Liverpool, the headquarters of the Blue Funnel Line.

This was my first trip by rail overnight, so I was glad of some cheery Royal Navy petty officer's who made sure I travelled in the right direction. In Liverpool, I was well received and told that I would be sent on a twenty-eight day "outward bound" course at Aberdovey – to make sure I was fit and able to take part in real-life boat drills.

Apparently, this had recently come about as a result of higher than normal deaths among first-trip midshipmen unlucky enough to get torpedoed. They explained that I could only sign-on if I passed all points of the course. The next available one was some time away, starting from November, the 20th to December, the 17th 1943. I passed and I signed my Blue Funnel indentures on 30 December 1943, for four years.

I now joined the 7644 grt *SS Glaucus* in Birkenhead, where she had just finished loading for Bombay with a full cargo of war materials. On the outward trip, we were in a convoy of eighty-five ships. Once clear of land, we thrust out into the Atlantic. My duties were as messenger for the first mate, who stood on the bridge during the four-to-eight watch. Our last sighting of Britain was the lighthouse of Inishtrahull. I was told, "Take a good look. It may be your last sight of land."

We soon reached deep water and headed south for Gibraltar. The ship next to us on our port side, two cables between ranks, was the ill-fated *Fort Stikine* — a Canadian built answer to the American liberty ships.

Deck Cadet Sturrock's sketch of SS Fort Stikine. The waves were eight to the mile.

Built 1943, 7154 grt dimensions: 134.72 x 17.37 x 10.6 m steel. Steam Triple expansion engines. 628 n.h.p., 11 knots, 5 inch (127 mm) stern gun, bow mounted 3 inch (76 mm) A.A., 8 x 20 mm A.A. Cannon. Torpedoed 1944.

Off the entrance to the Mediterranean, the convoy separated to allow different sections to sail for West Africa. We continued east and soon entered the Suez canal, where abundant war damage was visible, including a large cargo ship lying upright in the desert. She had been mined and couldn't be saved.

On docking at Bombay, now called Mumbai, it was time to unload *Glaucus's* cargo — mostly war materials for the Army.

One day, my chum and I reported smoke drifting out of number four tween deck. The third mate told us to man the winches as the stevedores rushed to abandon ship. We winched up the smoking drums and swung them over the side into the water to douse them. I can't say how long this situation lasted, but we finished discharging and learned the ship was to sail "in ballast" for Cape Town, then on to West Africa.

We arrived at the Cape to be greeted with the news of a huge explosion aboard the *Fort Stikine* in Bombay that had killed thousands and left her wreck lying on the top of a warehouse.

It could have been us!

Editor's note:

The Bombay Docks Explosion) of 14 April 1944.

The 7,142 ton freighter *SS Fort Stikine* carried a cargo of timber, cotton bales, barrels of oil, gold, torpedoes, ammunition, spitfires, and 1,400 tons of explosives. She caught fire and exploded in two giant blasts that sank nearby ships. Flying debris set the area ablaze, killing an estimated 800 — 1300 people.

The captain, Alexander James Naismith, who died in the explosion, had protested that the cargo was, "just about everything that will either burn or blow up". The ship had been waiting 48 hours for unloading.

When the fire was discovered, the crew and the local fire brigade made frantic efforts to extinguish it. The heat and smoke were overpowering. Sixteen minutes after the order to abandon ship, she blasted apart. Seismographs 1700 km distant recorded the earth tremor, the blast carried 50 miles, and windows shattered seven and a half miles away. Two square miles were set ablaze and thirteen ships sunk. Bombay and its people suffered severe damage. A Memorial stands outside Mumbai Fire Brigade Headquarters.

Sub-Lieutenant Ken Jackson, RNVR, and Chief Petty Officer Brazier were sent to Bombay on 7 May 1944 to assist the Indian Government in the salvage operation. Brazier was awarded the MBE and Jackson received an accelerated promotion, for their efforts.

Wartime censorship prevailed then, but I can't help thinking that Bill and his fellow deck cadet should have been commended for their alertness and subsequent bravery. I had direct experience of Bill's sharpness when he noticed a young boy cycling into danger from cars and, by now in his eighties, shouted a timely warning.

SS Fort Stikine and Bombay explosion aftermath with the Memorial erected outside Mumbai Fire Brigade Headquarters

1944 Bombay harbour explosion propeller piece

BELL ROCK & APPROACHES TO RIVER TAY & FORTH

As I kept my old wooden boat in Tayport Harbour, I became familiar with a whole family of major lighthouses. However, the bulk of my sailing was daytime only, including fishing trips to the Bell Rock.

Stormalong was an original "Falmouth Quay Punt" and was in very poor condition when I bought her "as seen" ashore at Tayport Harbour. I had several friends, ranging from shipwrights to fishermen, who were all experienced boat builders/repairers. They encouraged me to get stuck in to repairing and refitting my elderly boat. All these stout hearts were regular "tide watchers" who inhabited the Bell Rock Tavern. This was no great coincidence as my 1950 trip, from Tayport to Barbados was planned in the Bell Rock.

The entire shakedown trip and teething troubles were sorted out there as well. So in no time at all *Stormalong* acquired a nearly new air-cooled "Deutz" diesel engine that needed a marine gearbox. As there were numerous boatyards up and down the Fife and Angus coasts, I was able to acquire a second-hand one.

With advice from different engineers, I soon matched them up with a toothed Fenner belt drive that did a reasonable job.

Whilst all this was going on, I was lucky enough to find a full set of canvas sails from a local boat owner who had decided to re-rig as Bermudan. His gaff main had only been used for two seasons, was in near perfect condition, and represented a real bargain at £70. Once we had checked the entire hull planking, beefed up the stern post, and fitted a new cutlass bearing for the propeller shaft, it became a priority to launch *Stormalong* and test her new engine and gearbox.

At the time, only the inner end of Tayport Harbour was available for yachts. The sawmill used the bulk of the east side to berth laden timber ships. They came in at high water and squeezed their own weight of mud away from the wall as they settled down at low water. When they finished discharge and sailed for the Baltic they left huge ponds along the wall. We could stay afloat there all day. From these temporarily berths, we could leave the harbour at about half flood and motors out into the wide Tay Estuary, then head upstream for a few hours testing. After some minor adjustments to the engine mountings, we were satisfied that all was ready for a mini cruise. My older brother Forbes had had some yachting experience on a fair-sized yacht, and my two sons Andrew and David were keen to have a go. So we planned to nip to the Forth and see how we got on.

The wind was light, south westerly and the sea calm. Under engine, we left Tayport Harbour shortly after high water and made all plain sale. With light airs from South west and a strong ebb *Stormalong* made good progress down to the bar, and as there was no swell, we crossed with no bother and headed south for Fife Ness. The wind was steady at south-south west force two, so it was a leisurely trip. As we were in sight of the North Carr Lightship, and almost becalmed, we heated up our supper of scotch eggs and beans. This went down a treat.

It soon became apparent that we were not going to get far, and we didn't have our navigation lights fitted. They were aboard, but were not unpacked along with our new Taylor paraffin cooker. The boys were tired, so the mate and I decided to anchor close in to Cambo Sands. We could see the light on the May Isle almost in transit with the North Carr, so we fired up the "Iron Topsail" and headed in – taking soundings as we closed the shore. We rounded up and anchored in three fathoms (about five and a half metres) and felt quite pleased with our first trip!

As we were only a few miles from the North Carr Lightship, its beam flashing in through the windows and illuminating our cabin was an unforgettable experience. After a quiet night's sleep, we motored round to Elie to visit a baker for some rolls and bread. Having recently holidayed at North Berwick, my sons asked if we could visit Dunbar and have a swim – so off we went. The weather remained favourable and the engine behaved, so the mate headed for the easily seen ruins of Dunbar Castle, while I prepared lunch. When the mate said he couldn't see the entrance to the harbour, I stuck my head up and saw fine on our starboard bow the white walls of the open-air swimming pool, and suggested he head for that with care, as I was cooking.

At last, two fishing boats appeared out of a red sandstone cliff. WOW slowdown and approach slowly! The entrance to this spacious harbour opens right below the castle, and we soon tied up for lunch.

The harbour master had advised us that the local fishing fleet used the wall on the downside, so we would be safer on the wall opposite the entrance, but could expect to dry out! Oh well, that's not a problem. We had unwittingly arrived at the home of what became my favourite beer – Bell Haven. It was served in a tiny pub, almost on the pier, from wooden casks with spiles. Great!

While steaming around the world, we often dreamed about working near home. One topic came up fairly frequently: to be aboard a coaster tanker carrying bulk Guinness where it was tested regularly to ensure it carried alright!

We had a great break at Dunbar, and as the weather was still fine, we planned an early start and head home to Tayport in a "oner". During the afternoon somewhere off St Andrews, the mate, who was down in the main cabin rolling a smoke, suddenly called out "Bill, I can see the Bell Rock."

I looked out from our starboard beam and there it was, a tall sunlit, white tower. I acknowledged this by replying that it was in clear view about seven miles off our beam.

"Yes," came the reply, "but I can see it from here!"

I had no choice but to nip below to find that, as we rolled in a slow swell, a fine crack between the second and third plank was opening to about one and a half inches. A quick search showed that the mast stays were bolted to a heavy rib or frame, which just happened to be cracked right through. Well, that's not always seen in a calm harbour and it was a good bit above our normal waterline. It could be dealt with at home. As we rounded up at the Bar of Tay, it wasn't long before we were tied up snug in Tayport Harbour. I realised that we had been very lucky with the weather and needed to improve the good ship *Stormalong*.

One of my chums Tommy Fisk, who had a vast experience of maintaining wooden boats, helped me list the jobs that were urgently required to strengthen the hull. I made thin three-ply templates for two frames that would be fitted alongside the old ones.

In these days, we were lucky to have several boat builders not too far away along the Fife coast. So I set off with my templates and called in at J. Miller's boatyard at Anstruther. His foreman took me across the road to where they had stacks of sliced trees. I told them about our old boat, and he pulled out a curved plank about two and a half inches thick. I showed him how the bevel would need to fit the ship side, and in no time, I had two very stout new ribs. I then asked about galvanised nails, and we went back into the main building. It was fantastic: along with wooden hoops for thick masts, they had barrels full of nails and bolts. They proudly showed me wonderful photographs of the famous yachts they had built.

With *Stormalong* hauled out near the top of the slip, we could make a start. Over the next two years, we gradually rebuilt our lovely old boat, but this did not stop us having weekend trips to go fishing round the Bell rock, and some longer trips up and down the coast. When most of the main work was complete, we planned a trip to the Orkney Islands.

When Big Brother Forbes and I were enjoying our supper at anchor off Kings Barns, we had no idea that the May Isle Light was the very first light in Scotland, nor that it went all the way back to 1636. The Isle of May lies five miles off the Fife coast between Fife Ness and Crail. At one time, away back, it was gifted to the Bishop of Reading; it was fought over and all kinds of writs flew.

At another time, it was gifted to the Bishop of St Andrews after the famous victory of Bannockburn! The Isle of May returned to private ownership in 1636 when it was gifted to the Cunninghams of Barnes. They built the first tower, which had an iron brazier burning coal at the rate of about one ton a night. It worked okay in average weather, but in easterly gales the flames were blown horizontally shoreward and were invisible from seaward.

This changed when the new Commissioners Of Northern Lights took over in about December 1810. This came about because two naval ships, HMS Nymphe and Pallas, were wrecked near Dunbar. They had observed a lime kiln and mistook it for the May. As a result of this, the Northern

Lighthouse Board (NLHB) fitted oil lamps and reflectors in 1816.

The fruits of much labour: a seagoing boat

FIRST LONG VOYAGE NORTH

Heading for Orkney

We had completed all the jobs needed to make *Stormalong* seaworthy – having fitted her navigation lights and new "Taylors" pressure cooker. Yacht and crew now seemed ready for a longer voyage, so I bought some charts for the Orkney Islands. We planned to make it a two-week job, hoping to set off on Saturday 12th August 1972. The crew would be myself, big brother Forbes, and my two sons, Andrew and David.

All on board strained at the bit to head north, but we had left Tayport late, and didn't relish a night sail. So we anchored off Lucky Scalp Beacon for a quiet sleep. Next day saw our sails fill with a good breeze, which made us feel better, but *Stormalong* soon ran into fog – with visibility down to fifty-yards. We had reached Lunan Bay, so closed the shore and narrowly avoided the trap of some staked nets set to catch salmon. Straining eyes glimpsed a caravan near a sandy beach. We closed on it, and anchored in about four fathoms (about seven and a half metres), to await the fog clearing.

The crew awoke to an improving day and a clear, light breeze, allowing us to head for Scurdie Ness Lighthouse. We made good progress, reckoning to make Aberdeen before long. The entrance to "The Granite City" is well-marked by Girdle Ness Lighthouse. We rounded it at 17.00 and motored in. A rather pawky harbour assistant instructed us to tie up just past the fuel berth. The basin looked oily, with several tugs and floating pontoons – not exactly a yacht haven!

Back now in civilisation, we could visit shops and chandlers. After a run ashore and big eats, the crew turned in for a good night's sleep. Morning dawned, revealing a clear sky and moderate south-east breeze. We left after breakfast and headed for Peterhead's Slains Castle. The welcome sight of the lighthouse at Buchan Ness greeted us, and we motored into the "Harbour of Refuge" at Peterhead.

They created this harbour for the benefit of the Royal Navy's early steam battle wagons. It is very deep at the entrance – nine fathoms, (sixteen metres) – so I picked up a mooring buoy, to avoid the hustle and bustle of the inner harbour. Nowadays, there is a marina in the south corner of the big Harbour of Refuge.

Next day dawned with a light southerly breeze. The forecast promised more of the same, so we planned to sail out then head north for Fraserburgh. After a quick brew, we slipped our moorings and made all plain sail.

Rattray Head Lighthouse soon faded a couple of miles off our port beam. Not long after, the same happened to Carnbulg Beacon. From there, Fraserburgh Harbour hove into view as we sailed on. The harbour breakwater reaches out a long way. We rounded up just outside, handed all sail, started the engine, and motored on.

A friendly harbour master waved us in, requested we head to the north basin, and charged twenty-five pence! Over the years, I found these chaps very helpful, especially if it became necessary to leave a boat unattended for a long spell. We never planned to stay more than one night, but the weather clerk had other ideas. The forecast threatened strong north-west winds, so it seemed safer to stay put – it's a wide entrance to Moray Firth.

Can you see the bottom?

However, we spent some time exploring, and found Kinnaird Head Lighthouse fascinating – a cross between a museum and a shop – and well worth a visit. It was now the weekend. After watching a large ketch struggling to get round into the Moray Firth, it seemed wise to sit tight and await better conditions.

The following day brought a huge improvement. The forecast at 06.00 promised a south-west 4, so no times was lost before heading out to inspect the Moray Firth. We had enquired about good marks for fishing, and the friendly harbour master told us the best was quite close – a rocky bank known as the "Tankie". You found it by lining with a conspicuous fuel tank, which had a minor light, on the harbour entrance.

Stormalong motored out until the depth reduced. The bank proved fairly small, so the boat soon drifted over it, so the exercise had to be repeated. The mate (big brother) caught all the big fish. The weather had settled, so we pushed on to explore the Moray Coast.

Keen to visit as many harbours as possible, we popped into Port Soy. This predominately fishing harbour looks good, but is liable to dry out at low water, so we continued westward to Port Knockie – a spectacular little natural hole in the cliffs, and almost deserted. However, a local man reckoned the boat could stay afloat by lying alongside the outer wall. As low water was at 02.10, I decide to waken early to check it out – the yacht still floated – great!

After a lazy breakfast, we discussed what to do; our two-week holiday now half over. Big brother argued against trying to make any more northing. But I saw a yellow radar target buoy on the Moray Firth Chart, about halfway across to Lybster (about twenty miles). I convinced him that, if it could be reached in six, or less, hours, we should keep going. He agreed

The forecast was good – westerly 4, so we were under way by 08.30 and made all plain sail. Conditions proved excellent, and to the west appeared the major lighthouse at Covesea Skerries.

Visibility was above par at a range of fifteen miles We flew along like a fish on steroids. By 10.30 the wind rose to force six, justifying two reefs in the main. Our course for Lybster was 330°, taking us close to the Radar Buoy, which came abeam at 14.10. Both of us now agreed to keep going for Lybster, but the wind dropped, so we started the engine, and motor sailed.

Clyth Ness Lighthouse appeared, jutting out from the cliffs a few miles to the north, but it proved difficult to see the harbour entrance at Lybster. We handed all sails and proceeded with caution. On the north-east side the cliffs sloped down at a steep angle, looking like a huge roof. As we got closer, the sight of a group of waving fishermen cheered us up. They stood on the harbour wall opposite the sloping cliff. On our approach they shouted, "Keep close to the wall – the harbour entrance is about halfway." *Stormalong* found plenty of water and, as we neared the gap, the locals guided us in. They advised a turn to port, to avoid the shallow inner harbour.

These men directed us to a vacant berth, and took our ropes, saying they had worked as fishermen on a small vessel like ours. These good folk also offered us a carrier bag with half a dozen plump haddock. What a welcome!

We had logged thirty-eight miles across the Moray Firth, and still had hopes of making the Orkneys. Next day saw us on course for Wick, but struggling with gusty headwinds. Even well inshore, *Stormalong* heeled-over a fair bit when a strong gust came whistling out of a "GEO" (geothermal). On finally reaching Wick, we reckoned the Orkneys too far away, and made plans to head for home.

While ashore for stores, we discovered a shop selling Caithness Glass, so chose some bowls for souvenirs. On calling in at the harbour office to pay our dues, the large photographs showing the harbour full of fishing boats amazed us. The harbour master explained they dated from the height of the herring boom, some fifty years earlier. What a contrast; our boat looked like the only one in!

It seemed like a good idea to visit as many small ports as possible while heading down towards the head of the Moray Firth, for future reference.

As the winds proved light and variable, we motor-sailed down towards the "Ord of Caithness" where the cliffs seemed to plunge right into the sea. We obtained fixes from "Latheron Wheel" and "Dunbeath Castle" but didn't bother trying to enter, as it looked difficult. Our next stop would be Helmsdale, which looked good, but the forecast was for north-west 5-6, so we made all plain sail and soon flew along towards Tarbat Ness Lighthouse. It guards the entrance to the Dornoch Firth and looks very cosy, but it is very shallow. We left it to starboard and headed down to Wilk Haven, two miles further on.

According to the mate, Lord Carnegie had a large steam yacht too big to enter the Firth or to steam up to Skibo (his luxury home) so he had a slip built at Wilk Haven. There, his yacht anchored off and his guests found carriages awaiting.

After a good tuck in, we told the boys to play around with the dinghy (it was now a flat calm) while we walked to Portmahomack, about three miles away, to phone home. The age of mobile phones hadn't caught up with us. After locating a public kiosk, we made our calls then started for Wilk Haven. By now, pitch-black night had fallen. Nearing the shore, we heard the boys chatting, but couldn't see a sign of the boat. I realized the importance of showing an anchor light: to help find *Stormalong*, and protect her. However, she sat where left and in no time her galley lit up and the kettle sang its siren song.

Next morning, we rose early. The forecast promised west four to five, so we decided to get under way and eat later. With all plain sail and a calm sea, we soon flew along at six knots – this is what we had signed on for! Our destination – Fraserburgh, about sixty miles down wind.

10.55 saw us approaching the major lighthouse at Covesea Skerries, and still flying along. At mid-day, Bin Hill rose abeam, with twenty-two miles logged – not bad, and definitely the best sail so far. We ticked off our positions on the chart, flying past the ports visited on our way north. First, Port Knockie; then, White Hills, and at 17.50 *Stormalong* pulled abreast of Troup Head. The sea rose and the helm felt a bit heavy, so we pulled down a reef to shorten sail. At 18.30, off Rosehearty, problems increased. The sea surged with menacing overfalls – but we could cope. By 19.00 Kinnaird Head Lighthouse came abeam, enabling us to see Fraserburgh.

Stormalong flew before the wind, and at 19.15 we could "gybe oh" and head in to Fraserburgh. 19.30 found us tied up in the Balaclava Basin, with sixty miles under sail and one by engine – sixty-one miles logged. After a long lie, followed by a full breakfast, the crew drifted ashore to top up supplies.

The forecast promised a north-east three to four, so, after motoring out, we set all plain sail and headed for home. Around midday the lighthouse on Rattray Head was passed, and everything looked fine. 14.25 found us abeam of Buchan Ness, and heading for Stonehaven. At 15.36 we passed Slains Castle (inspiration for Dracula) and by 18.00 the wind fell light, so it was "engine on" and head in for Stonehaven. We moored *Stormalong* in the outer harbour, and called it a good day.

Now some forty-odd miles from home, we could take a break and leave early. Catching the flood tide when approaching the Bar of Tay seemed like a good idea. So, on our last day, the crew rose at 06.00 and downed a cup of tea, before motoring out to find a wind. The forecast was variable, so it seemed best to motor-sail down towards Tod Head – where they had promised good fishing.

Some sizeable codling soon wriggled aboard. Then, with a light breeze from south-east, we set all plain sail and fixed a course for the Red Head. This famous landmark comes to life if you can plan to pass about five miles off at sunrise.

WOW! They glow blood-red – but in daytime, they are all quite dull. Anyway, we now had them abeam at 15.00, and aimed to arrive at the Abertay about 17.25 – which meant catching the flood tide all the way up to Tayport.

By 20.10, *Stormalong* lay at her moorings, having done 401 miles by the log – 150 by engine, and 251 by sail.

A good trip, but we had failed to make the Orkneys.

Stormalong: a beautiful sight

Entrepreneur

Editor's note:

Having survived the rigours of Aberdovey and tough years at sea, Bill developed the capacity to tackle every and any task that came his way. While running The Firth of Lorne Sea School, he decided to have a business calendar and, being a canny Scot, saved a groat or two by using his own drawings.

Tarbat Ness Lighthouse

Knowing how much the Princess Royal loves lighthouses, and having been trained by the same Kurt Hahn's principles as her father (another old wartime seadog) Bill thought to send Princess Anne a copy. He was delighted to receive a reply.

BUCKINGHAM PALACE

15th July 2009

Dear Captain Sturrock,

The Princess Royal has asked me to thank you for your recent letter and for enclosing a copy of your Tarbat Ness Lighthouse calendar. Her Royal Highness was very touched by your kind thoughts in writing and sending her the calendar, and she sends you and your family her best wishes for the future.

Yours sincerely
Nick Wright

Captain Nick Wright, LVO, Royal Navy
Private Secretary to
HRH The Princess Royal

Captain W. Sturrock

When he wasn't building boats, turning bowls on a lathe, shooting, fishing and gardening, in the evening he used rope skills picked up at sea to good effect.

And seeing as you asked, yes, he does enjoy a dram. And, no, he didn't distil it himself.

FOUR-WEEK TRIP TO TOBERMORY

Mermaids

In July of 1973, the Sturrock clan intended to nip up to the Moray firth and visit some new places on the way to Inverness and the Caledonian Canal. We had learned from last year's trip that more time was needed if we were to visit somewhere new. The intention was to allow four weeks to achieve our plans.

On Tuesday, July 24, we set off with three weeks of stores and a full crew. The plan was to hop up to Aberdeen and round Kinnaird's Head and on to Lossiemouth, which we approached on Wednesday, 1 August. However, when in sight of the harbour, about 6 miles to the south-west of our position, at 07.30 the breeze died and the engine refused to start. The battery was flat.

Stormalong

We were now coasting slowly towards the harbour entrance, so, after breakfast, we talked David into towing us in by rowing the dinghy. Now quite close to the entrance, I told David, we would attach a long rope so he could reach the harbour steps and make us fast. He made it ashore and we pulled ourselves in. There was no garage to charge the battery, so I phoned to arrange a car to take us home. With a full charge, we returned the following night, and the next day my son and I motored out to a light, southerly breeze and headed for the Inverness Firth.

We entered Clachnaharry Sea Loch and tied up at Muirtown Basin at Inverness. It was the start of the Caledonian Canal and dues had to be paid before proceeding further. After a walk ashore, we sampled some malt whisky, in case our journey was wet. It also helps to keep the skipper from getting miserable if he gets wet.

Before going anywhere, the tank needed a fill up with diesel as we would most likely have to motor most of the 50-odd miles to Fort William. I had been told that there was a fuel depot quite close, so I set off to find it. As I approached, a big tanker was about to leave, so I waved him down to ask if he could sell a tank full. He asked where we were tied up, saying he was going to a fishing boat further up and would come back to us.

I was not long returned to the boat when the tanker appeared. He was quite *joco* as his call had ordered a full load, but could only take about half. Unable to take it back, he was quite happy to give us a great deal. Unfortunately, he pumped it so fast that David, who was holding the delivery hose, had a blowback and got his eye full of diesel.

We sailed down to the Muirtown Basin at Achnacarry and entered the four sisters of the canal, then Dochgarroch Loch, which is part of the canal. We proceeded onwards to the anchorage at Loch Dochgarroch, had lunch, and then launched the dinghy to go fishing. The next stage took us into Loch Ness, and towards Castle Urqhart, which was sheltered from the South West breeze, to anchor in five fathoms

Sitting pretty

After supper, we went ashore to walk to Drumnadrochit, but found it was too far from the boat (eight miles). Next morning after breakfast, we weighed anchor and headed for Fort Augustus, and then into Invermoriston for lunch. From here it wasn't far to Fort Augustus, where we tied up alongside as the locks had closed for the night.

We were up early the next morning, and, after a quick breakfast, entered the first lock along with a big Nicholson yacht called *Gailliard*. We left the top lock bound for Loch Oich, about two and a half miles away. We had reached the summit of the canal by climbing fourteen locks and it was all downhill now, past Invergarry Castle. Arrived at Laggan Lock led to the lovely

Laggan Avenue, with its magnificent trees, 32 metres above sea level. The big house at Achnacarry was once the main training headquarters for the commandos.

After Laggan came Loch Lochy and anchorage at Achnacarry Bay. We left Loch Lochy at Gairlochy. From here the course was for Banavie Locks (eight down) to the entrance at Corpach Sea Lock (Neptune's ladder). We motored across Loch Linnie and anchored at Camus Na Gall in heavy rain. After lunch, via Corran Narrows led to Kentallan Bay on Lismore, where we anchored for the night. It was really cold and felt like the Arctic.

Next morning saw us depart Kentallan for Craignure on Mull, where we anchored and went to the pub. During the night, I awoke to a noise like rushing water, and scrambled out of my bunk, fearing the worst! What a shock – we were completely surrounded by a huge shoal of mackeral leaping out of the water in panic.

I had left my sea rod against the mast and lost no time in casting. We soon had a good catch of these oily fish. Suddenly, they all disappeared! I guess they had been attacked by a large predator, but what luck for us! Later that morning, we headed up the Sound of Mull towards Tobermory, and had a great breakfast of fresh fish on the way. A good catch

We arrived in the bay, went ashore, and met up with the crew of the Nicholson, who had come through the first lock on the canal with us. Later that night, we were awakened by the anchor dragging in a force-eight gale, so moved to Aros Bay for shelter. Once the gale had eased, we moved back to Tobermory.

The following day we left for Oban and anchored off the Great Western Hotel. David went ashore and went adrift. The crew looked everywhere, but couldn't find him. We had to contact the police, who conducted a search.

Eventually, he turned up on the beach, and told us he had gone to the cinema. Although we were angry with him, at the

same time it was a relief that he was okay. The next day we left
Oban and headed home to Tayport.

Stormalong in full sail

FASTNET DISASTER AVOIDED

The owner of the yacht *Sanda* decided to sell his house in Fife and move to a West Coast one at Loch Goil — up Loch Long, in the Clyde area.

We were asked to move his boat over to Loch Goil and to run it as a trip boat. Our first venture was planned for the 11th of August. The crew were keen to start, so we loaded up and motored out to head down to Holy Loch and Hunter's Quay.

This is a popular stop for yachtsmen, and we were soon exploring ashore. Our plan was to visit the Isle of Arran, which has several good anchorages. Next day, we got underway early and headed down to pass between the Cumbrae Islands and the Isle of Bute.

I had already experienced some excellent sea fishing out of Largs and around the Cumbrae's, but not this time. We headed south for Arran, whose mountains were now unmistakable. Brodick Bay was our goal, which lay about ten miles ahead. On arrival, we decided to keep going as the shelter was not as good as I would have liked. From the chart and pilot book, we felt Holy Isle, at the entrance of Lamlash, appeared to be a better bet. So we carried on, admiring the scenery of Arran's mountains. On rounding Holy Isle, we found the anchorage quite comfortable and dropped anchor for the night.

The following day, we decided to head west to Campbeltown and soon came up to Pladda Lighthouse. This coincided with the Clyde coastguard coming alive and enquiring if we had received the forecast. "Yes," we told him, but it was not as we had hoped, with its strong winds. We said we would return to Lamlash, and he reckoned we were right.

Stirring Seas

Back at Lamlash, which we felt was a very sheltered spot, some of us headed ashore. I decided to phone home as none of us had mobiles. I shall never forget my wife's response.

"Thank God you are safe."

"Why?" I replied.

"Because three hundred and three yachts racing to Fastnet have been badly hit by severe gales with five yachts sunk, nineteen abandoned and 15 crewmen lost."

We did not find out all the details then and there, but as our weather had started to improve, it was decided to press on to Campbeltown, round Arran, and then home.

Editors note:

Rescue operations were ongoing from 14-16 August. 303 yachts started, 19 abandoned and 5 sunk.

15 crew lost, 7 of those from life rafts although the abandoned yachts were subsequently recovered. 6 lives were lost through the failure of safety harnesses.

979mb depression, 50-60 knot gusts at peak of the storm.

112 yachts reported that they were knocked down to horizontal during the storm.

HOME RUN

The Pentland Firth has been much feared by mariners over the years because of its strong tides. These can run up to seven knots on springs, and proved a real barrier to an invading Roman fleet. As the legions struggled northwards, they depended on the ships for supplies. Unable to cope with such strong tides, the campaign fizzled out – and the army retreated behind Hadrian's Wall.

Nowadays, we are better informed, with clear tidal information to help us cope with strong streams. According to the Clyde Cruising Club Sailing Directions, avoid these four conditions – swell, spring tides, wind against tide, and wind over force four.

Running a sailing school on the West Coast of Scotland all summer, while living on the East Coast, meant a hectic dash to get the yacht round in the spring. And then another mad dash in the autumn so that we could resume our evening classes in October.

The previous year, our plans to come home via the Pentland Firth had been thwarted by winds of force ten and eleven. They pinned us down in Loch Linnhe over a weekend, on anchor watch, with no way of getting ashore. In the end we cut our losses, ran up Loch Linnhe for the Caledonian Canal and took the easy way home.

Now, a year later, we had a much better forecast and everything looked good. I had a diver scrub my yacht *Sula's* bottom to make sure we would not be sluggish.The growth had been very heavy owing to a high sea temperature and strong sunlight. We had stores for a week and our tanks were full. As soon as the crew came aboard (two Johns one Jack and a Nick, all having sailed with me before) we decided on a quick dash to Tobermory.

The plan was, as usual, based on tides. If we caught the first of the flood at Ardnamurchan point, then we could expect to arrive at Kyle Rhea Narrows, inside Skye, at slack water. This is a very important tidal exercise. Getting it wrong would mean a six hour delay in the Sound of Sleat, where the streams run up to eight knots.

We motored out of Loch Creran, and set the full main and No1 jib, the wind being SW3. *Sula* felt lively and responsive, and was obviously enjoying the freedom provided by a clean bottom. We joked and swapped stories of our earlier trips, in eager anticipation of the week ahead.

We soon set the Genoa and sailed for the Sound of Mull, which we entered at 1900. By 19.30, it was dark, and low cloud told of rain – not unusual for a SW wind in these parts. However, the Sound of Mull is so well lit with sector lights and buoys that we refer to it as Piccadilly Circus.

I was having my usual forty winks when Nick asked me to come on deck as there was some doubt about whether or not we had arrived at the entrance to Tobermory Bay. Remembering that none of the crew had been that way for some time, I stuck my head out and told them we were almost past the entrance, and if they didn't go about we would not get our short stay ashore.

We anchored quite close to Bobby McLeod's Fifer and were soon ashore – reporting our progress on the phone and having a farewell drink with friendly barmaids and fishermen, who always make Tobermory a worthwhile stop. Nick and John were determined that sleep wasn't going to interfere with their fun. After ferrying the rest of us back to the yacht, I informed them that in order to catch the tide they must be aboard no later 01.45. They then returned ashore.

It seemed that I had no sooner got my head down when they were clattering around on deck deflating the dinghy and putting the kettle on. Underway at 02.10, we had a drizzle and gusty southerly winds making it rather miserable for the watch, but keeping our speed up around the five knot mark.

Off Ardnamurchan, we decided to hand the main and keep the No1 jib up as the sea was lumpy, making steering difficult. I always like to stay at least two miles off the Point to avoid the backlash of rebounding seas, however, on this occasion it made little difference as the sea was very confused. At 04.15 Ardnamurchamn Light was abeam and the tide flooding for the next six hours.

I had another forty winks, and soon heard that the light on Eillan Castle off Eigg was abeam. We had marked our position on the chart at required points in the time scale of our plan, and this was bang on 05.45. Visibility was very poor and no more lights of any consequence until Sleat Point and the loom of Mallaig. As daylight crept reluctantly in, we passed Armadale and all was well. *Sula* now rolled along with the wind aft, so we hoisted full main and entered Kyle Rhea Narrows with about five minutes in hand – and seventeen minutes later organised a hearty breakfast.

Now the land closed in on both sides and we had hardly any time to identify Gavin Maxwell's cottage, tucked in behind

Sandaig Lighthouse. Our main concern was to reach Glenelg and the Southern entrance to Kyle Rhea before the tide turned against us. All was well, and the dreaded overfalls were hardly noticeable as we sliced into the narrows. From start to finish it is only two miles, but so narrow it is reminiscent of the famous *Culebra Cut* in the Panama Canal.

To celebrate our delight with the progress so far, it was decided to stay at Kyle and eat properly. Kyleakin Pier is an ideal spot for a yacht. We found a nice, big, wooden fishing boat and tied up alongside her, and ate well from a cold roast and vegetables. So far we had broken all our own records and had covered ninety-two miles in fifteen and a half hours, so we felt well pleased with the way things were going.

At 12.30, we took off again to head for Acarseid. Mhor in South Rhona, halfway up the inner sound, taking the sheltered route inside Skye. As so often happened, the geography upset the wind and we now found ourselves beating with a WNW four to five. By now we had one reef in the main and the No 2 Jib. By 14.45, the wind was light so we had the engine on and motored up the last twelve miles to one of the best little anchorages there is – Acarseid Mhor, which means " Big Harbour". At this time of year, deserted – and nobody felt like spoiling it by going ashore, so we cracked a bottle of wine (actually a three litre box) and sat back to enjoy the scenery. The autumn colours amongst the surprising stands of beech and conifers look out of place in such a rocky place. We contemplated a good sleep.

The next stage was to make for Ullapool and rest again before Cape Wrath. We turned in, setting the alarm for an early forecast. This worked out in our favour, giving Southerly five to six all round the Hebrides and Minches. We soon got underway only to discover no wind at all. The log shows calm until 11.30 when, having motored monotonously for nearly five hours, we were suddenly headed with a northerly breeze. Oh well, shut off the engine and get on with beating. This soon assumed alarming proportions

Cape Wrath Lighthouse

As the breeze worsened to a rumbustious six to seven, we were getting quite good at changing down headsails and reefing. As no mention of this wayward wind appeared at the 13.50-hour forecast, I started looking for other options – a rising wind always seems to make the worst sea for heading into. Loch Inver was almost abeam on our starboard side and we decided that would have to do.

We felt rather tame anchoring at 1600 having only done fifty-four miles, and thirty of that under engine, but the prospect of beating against that cold northerly was not so good. We took the opportunity of "bending on" our new mainsail for the hard sail ahead. Loch Inver is a pleasant little place and pub friendly. We went ashore for a stretch, and then had a serious planning session for the next day.

Once again the tides were uppermost in our minds, and by a stroke of good fortune, we were well placed to scoop the tidal pool. By leaving at 0400 the next morning, we hoped to carry the north-going stream until almost mid-day, then the east-going stream beginning at Cape Wrath. By using our new average speed of five knots, we would be there at the right time to catch it all the way along the north coast. After our evening meal, we decided on an early night and set the alarm for 0400.

Tuesday 04.30 hrs.

After an early cup of tea, we found the fishing fleet getting under way. It was decided to follow them out, but they used a shortcut inside a small rocky island, so we chose to use the same route as when arriving.

Once outside, we found that the unwanted northerly had given way to a gentle southerly, so, at 05.30 we made full sail. The speed built up to five and a half on the clock and soon Stoer Head Light lay abeam. Daylight was slow to arrive, and it was drizzling again – visibility varied between three to five miles. We didn't see much of the mainland, glimpsing Handa Island, with its sheer cliffs, as it came abeam after breakfast.

We were now going along at a good six knots and had Cape Wrath abeam at 11.30, but stood on to avoid the off-lying rocks. Our luck was in, the drizzle stopped and the low overcast was replaced by a higher level of cloud. Visibility was much better now and we could see all the way along the north coast of Scotland.

Nearest to us was Whiten Head, so called for its pale coloured cliffs. Beyond lay Strathay Point and Dunnet Head. To the north east the Orkneys were showing, with the Old Man of Hoy clearly visible. We made a ritual of fixing our position at noon, and altered course to eastward, hardening up our sheets. *Sula* really got her shoulder down and showed us how to get on with eating up the miles.

Mid afternoon, the wind eased off somewhat, but nor for long. We soon had a reef in the main and changed down to the No 2 jib. The wind being off the land, we had ideal sailing conditions and were able to admire the scenery in Loch Eribol. Ben Hope slid past, followed by Kyle of Tongue and Ben Loyal. I was able to point out some secluded beaches where we had spent family holidays and were able to read a newspaper at midnight in July, on the shore.

By 1620 we were of Strathay Point Lighthouse and were taking bearings on Dounreay's massive silver sphere. By 1730, we logged the wind as southerly seven to eight and were making plans for arriving at Scrabster. Of course, as we rounded Holburn Head the wind veered to the west giving us a beat up into the bay as we approached Scrabster Harbour. We tied up to an old converted RNLI Lifeboat in the inner harbour.

We all felt that we had really experienced a fantastic day's sail, logging ninety-six miles at an average six-point-four knots. The pub in Scrabster was probably the least charming of our watering holes, but we didn't care. The crew toasted everything and everybody in the safe knowledge we didn't have to get up early. On this occasion, the tides really did dictate our time of departure because on the morrow we were going through the Pentland, where only fools rush in!

Wednesday

After breakfast, I sought out the harbour master to pay our dues, and he confirmed that 11.00-12.00 would be a suitable time to leave. He also mentioned that he had spoken to Pentland Coastguard who had added his three penny worth (*you'll have an exciting trip but it is reasonable to carry on.*) I was suitably assured. We decided on 11.00 as it would take about one hour to clear Thurso Bay, and the tide was predicted to run eastward from just after mid-day.

The crew were on deck making preparations to leave when I heard voices having some sort of exchange. They sounded like strangers, so I popped out on deck. Two young fishermen were trying to persuade us that it was unwise to attempt Pentland so early, as the tides were not behaving according to the Admiralty predictions. Intrigued, I tried to discover the source of this difference of opinion, as I was convinced a strong SW wind would bring forward the start of the east-going stream.

"No, sir," the local lads retorted, "it's a lot later." On mentioning our tidal calculations and the harbour master's corroboration they simply replied, "You can throw the tide tables out the window – the tides are all to hell right now!"

Well, this was a horse of another colour. I didn't feel like throwing away all our deliberations without at least a token struggle, so I answered somewhat smugly that I would have to check this out with an expert. Namely, one Denny Simpson, the skipper of a local fishing boat that was in port at the time and whom I was fairly acquainted with. This drew hoots of laughter from our local pair; "He's our father," was the reason for the mirth.

However, having made up my mind, I decided to check it out. We motored across the bay and lay alongside *Pavonia,* a sturdy wooden fishing boat that worked the northern waters, and whose skipper was probably one of the best sources of local information I could hope to find. He professed to be somewhat baffled himself, saying that high-water Liverpool was the best guide for the Pentland.

After consulting his tables, he stated it would be safe after twelve noon. He also threw in some very useful information about the pilotage of the Pentland, which we were glad of later "It's hold out into the Firth until halfway across to Orkney, then head for the church on Stroma. That way you will clear a nasty counter-current that runs west from Dunnet Head across the bay. When you get close to Stroma, the Merry Men of Mey will be abeam to starboard and you can head for John O' Groats – the stream will carry you through clear of all dangers".

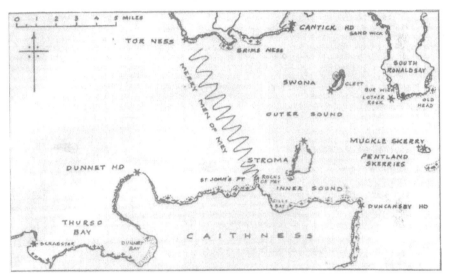

The Merry men of Mey

We thanked Denny for his help, and delayed our departure for half an hour as a precaution, making doubly sure that all was well secured before departing Scrabster at 11.30. We now found that a large swell had built up from the west since we arrived, so we hoisted No 2 Jib with a reef in it and kept the mainsail secured. Yet we were still logging five and a half knots and soon clearing Holburn Head, with the swell growing bigger all the time. So big

– 49 –

that the P &.O. Ferry, about three miles away, was quite literally disappearing from sight between the crests.

By 1200, we were acutely aware of the fact that the tide still ran strongly to the west. Our bearings from Dunnet Head changed only very slowly and the swells began to break heavily. We had logged the wind as SW five to six – but these big Atlantic swells still curled over and broke along both sides of *Sula* as she surfed down their forward slopes at speeds of up to eight knots. The biggest ones looked quite spectacular and the noise they made sounded like an express train rushing out of a tunnel.

Sula

The crew were all hooked-on in the cockpit, with a lot of white knuckles in evidence I doubted if anyone would volunteer to go on the fore deck! Our helmsman was Nick, the youngest of the crew. Sitting just behind him, I asked if he could devote all his attention to keeping her head before the wind and not looking aft, as it was a little unnerving at times. By 12.45 we were absolutely convinced that our young friends in Scrabster were 100% right. We were obviously not making any real ground eastwards as Dunnet Head was still abeam. I was very glad that the tides were neaps.

The Stream Atlas showed three point seven as a rate then, quite suddenly, the sea began to smooth out and we started making ground at a noticeable speed. Very soon we could make out the details on Stroma and, at last, pick out the church we were supposed to be aiming for.

Stroma Lighthouse

At 13.50 we had the obvious Men of Mey Rocks abeam in a welter of white water and we altered round to 150°. Our log showed over seven knots, but our ground speed was over eleven – so we could only glance to port and starboard and register fleeting glances of points of interest as the shore flashed past. In no time at all, we had Duncansby Head Lighthouse abeam and the Pentland Skerries on our port bow.

Pentland Skerries

We now needed to beat south to Wick, so we hoisted our main and pulled in the third reef as the wind was now SW seven to eight, gusting nine. *Sula* leapt forward. The wind was off the land, so there was practically no sea. Our course was 180° (M) and we covered thirteen miles in two hours and ten minutes – tying up in Wick's huge, empty basin just after 17.00.

We felt there was a good case for fish supper and pint catering, so no time was wasted in getting ashore to check out these facilities. Our team of now-experienced navigators had already worked out that we needed an early start again, yes 05.30. We didn't stay ashore too long, but managed to visit several friendly pubs and learned of other visitors from Tayport who had celebrated their farthest north trip that summer. We were certainly all much more relaxed and the remainder of the trip was definitely going to be a piece of cake.

Thursday

We motored out, and found the wind still SW six, but low cloud and drizzle made the prospect a bit grim. We had Clyth Ness Light abeam, and at 06.12, doing seven knots with visibility moderate, we sped away SE for Fraserborough. The land at that part of the mainland is all low lying. I aimed further west for Troup Head to be sure not to miss our land-fall. Just after 0700, we were glad to see, blearily through the murk, the flare-off from the Beatrice oil field.

Our breakfast was shambolic – bowls of cereal handed out to the cockpit simply few away or filled up with salt spray, so we settled for a couple of hard boiled eggs! *Sula* cruised along at a steady eight knots, with sheets of spray thrown up from her weather bow driving across the length of the boat as she heeled to a beam wind. By now, we were taking bearings of Troup Head and soon had Kinnairds Head in sight. The wind had moderated so we shook-out the reefs and bent on the No 1 jib to maintain our best speed.

We rounded Kinnairds Head at 1500 and started reaching down to Rattray Head – that most dreaded of all East Coast headlands with its notorious tide rips. However, we had no trouble on this occasion and had her abeam in an hour and a quarter. From then on, we were heading down to Peterhead (of the giant fish suppers) and entered the harbour of refuge at 1900 to tie up shortly afterwards in the innermost of all the basins, almost a mile further in. Surrounded by hundreds of fishing boats, the sudden serenity was quite a contrast.

Friday

Somewhat of an anti-climax, as the wind went light and we were forced to motor-sail for about five hours until off Stonehaven. There, the wind returned with some more souths in it and we made five knots with the Genoa and full main. A long session of beating down the Sawtooth Coast on a mean course of 210°, with long legs on port, followed. When off Arbroath at 2100, the wind began to veer to WSW and gave us a glorious reach up the river Tay in the dark, with all the amber lights from Fife Ness to St Andrews and round to Carnoustie glittering like a giant necklace.

All hands came on deck and a couple of drams were due as the buoys were passed in short order. We tied up to a brand new Ferro Schooner. The owner was sleeping aboard and was some-what dismayed at the speed with which we made fast and headed off for the Bell Rock Tavern to celebrate. As he was a newcomer to the harbour, I assured him that we would be back later. Then I left to join the crew in a grand celebration of what was regarded as a record passage.

Bell Rock

Bell Rock Lighthouse

REACH FOR THE SKYE

The 1997 sailing season was not notable for gales or strong winds, at least not until September, which coincided with our last trip.

Some crew members had sailed with us before, and the newcomers were all keen to gain experience and make meaningful passages if possible. With that in mind we did a short hop on Saturday evening, after the usual session of stowing food, checking safety gear, then picking up a swinging mooring at Cragnuire, Mull. This also allowed a visit to the inn so that we could spend Saturday night ashore being sociable, instead of anchoring somewhere quiet

Back aboard it was planned to make the best of the broadcast SW4 on Sunday and head up for Canna, with a reasonably early start. This was somewhat forced on us by a nasty chop springing up around 07.00 with a moderate S-SE breeze, making Craignure less than pleasant.

So, after a cup of tea, we were on our way and soon anchored at Fishnish for a proper Sunday breakfast. From then on, we reeled off the miles at an average five knots to Canna. We arrived in good time for dinner and decided to leave the shore visit until the morning.

> Note:Although Canna did not have its own Harbour approach lights, we had our own system. After rounding the minor lights on the east point of Sanday Isle we kept off the nasty reef, Sgeir-A-Phuirt that lies two cables off the north shore of Sanday and dries out. By evening we approached the conspicuous headland Rhuba Carrunis and slowed down. When it's dark, the glow of the Major Lights at Hysgeir is clearly visible above the low lying isle of Sanday. When it comes in line with the silhouette of the conspicuous church, it makes a perfect transit, which is safe to head for. Watch the echo sounder as the depths reduce. This unusual transit does not appear on any chart or pilot book, but is caused by Hysgeir being a very powerful light with a range of 24 nautical miles. Having slowed down, it is now important to watch Ruba Carriniss fall back and the cottages and farm appear. Now, there might be other vessels at anchor, so care is needed.

After breakfast, we had a good walk around, wished the McKinnon family a quiet winter and hoped to see them all again next year.

The forecast was now a bit like the norm, with talk of SW4 backing to SSE5-6, and seven by evening, which made Barra less than inviting. But if the crew felt equal to it we could continue north with a view to circumnavigating Skye.

They were warned that we might get stuck somewhere and be late back, but that didn't seem to be too much of a problem. By heading for the north end of South Uist we could have good shelter and be well placed for continuing round Skye.

Loch Skiport is just such a place and the Wizard Pool is very snug, enclosed between the Wizard Isles and the Uist shore in the lee of Hecla. So we headed for Ushenish, the major light on the East Coast of South Uist, which is very conspicuous on a huge headland on this course. We were crossing the entrance of the "Little Minch" and soon could see another major light on Neist Point on Skye. As it was daylight, lights were not needed, and we soon reached the entrance to Loch Skiport and our destination of the Wizard Pool.

The crew ate well and slept soundly, undisturbed by the rising wind. We rose early and were advised by the coastguard of a new gale warning for sea areas Malin and Hebrides, SE8 expected soon.

Thinking *there is no going back now lads*, we decided to run under a small jib for the shelter of Loch Snizort. This great sheet of water is about twelve miles long by six miles wide and lies SE/NW of the Ascrib Islands, about halfway down.

It has half-a-dozen good anchorages plus the ferry terminal at Uig with shops etc. and is a very sheltered stretch of water that never feels the Atlantic swell. You are much more likely to meet whales here than yachts. My own favourite Anchorage is Aros Bay on the south shore, but you will have to go and see for yourself.

Our exit from Skiport was exciting, pushing through the onshore chop we already had three reefs in the main although the wind was only registering twenty-four knots, so we were a little under canvassed at first. That, however, sorted itself out as it soon piped up to thirty – thirty-five knots and we surfed along at about seven knots. Just here the Little Minch is about twelve miles wide and we had about twenty miles to Waternish Point.

Freya had the wind on her starboard quarter and was remarkably dry as we rolled along in great style. Weather conditions proved ideal with blinks of sun, tumbling white horses, and green seas, until we rounded Waternish Point and commenced to beat.

The gusts off the cliffs heeled us over and our speed dropped. So, it was on with the engine and soon we could see our destination.

It was time for a meal as breakfast had largely been missed and, of course, once we had eaten we convinced ourselves that the wind had dropped and that we could keep going around the top! This coincided with the forecast for the wind to veer from Southeast to Southwest and drop by evening – and it did.

The run up to Island Trodday was fast and smooth with the wind off the land. Up past Duntulm and through to the Inner Sound the wind dropped to a five and then disappearing altogether as we anchored in Staffin Bay.

So far so good, but we still had a lot of southing to make!

Anchored in calm water with the lights of Staffin reflected, it was difficult to remember how different it had been only a few hours before!

Wednesday arrived and we were just over halfway home so we set off early again, beating down the mainland shore with a southerly breeze. Some hard work followed, with short tacks until 16.20 when the shelter of Puldomhain just south of Applecross beckoned for a quick anchor and lunch.

Our Lucky Day

 Our luck was in because when we re-emerged the wind had veered to Southwest six. This gave us a cracking sail into Kyleakin where we picked up a visitor's mooring in a mirror-like calm. The bright lights of numerous pubs tempted us ashore, where we had a fantastic unwinding session in the company of back-packers from all over the world.

The real ale was good and there was a disco too, so we didn't get back aboard till the wee sma' hours, after a hilarious water battle as we attempted to board the inflatable. We were now three quarters of the way round Skye and gave ourselves a pat on the back!

At this juncture, we had to make a quick stop at Kyle to allow one of the crew away as it looked as if we were not going to make Oban on Friday. An early start didn't quite happen and we motored over to the railway pier, paid a quick visit to the shops and saw our crewman onto the train.

The tides were OK, but to make sure we motor-sailed through the Kings Kyle and entered the Sound of Sleat with 35 knots of wind and horrendous overfalls. Being mindful of the Shallow Spit on the Skye shore we had to stand well out into real nasty, white, tumbling overfalls.

As soon as we could see the shallows were abaft our beam, we tacked round and started to make some ground. Shortly after, we were able to lengthen our tracks and put the engine off. This was exciting stuff: we had to hang on to stay in the boat.

The brigantine *Jean de La Lune* appeared, stern standing on end, and burying her bowsprit. We called her on the VHF and heard that they could only make two knots in these conditions. We were able to keep up with her for a good hour.

At this point, it is worth remembering what the Admiralty Pilot says about Kyle Rhea. Apparently, one off their own survey ships had a very nasty experience whilst steaming south against a northerly current at revolutions of 12 knots: "no headway made". She was swung through 70 degrees and narrowly avoided running aground.

Although this was the shortest leg of our voyage, we all reckoned it was the most strenuous. With the wind at SW37 knots we decided Isle Oronsay looked too good to pass, so we jinked in and closed up to the village end of the bay, anchoring in 3.2m to 30m (all chain)

We heard JDL reporting his arrival at Ardvasar, but he switched off before we could call him. However, Cubby McKinnon, the skipper of Cuma, lying in Mallaig, answered: "I can't recommend Mallaig Bill, it's hell in here." So we stayed put. However, he put in a call to base on our behalf advising that we might have to abandon the cruise at Armadale on Friday and come home by ferry or train! Anyway, we were snug and well fed, but had to stand anchor watches until daybreak.

After a hearty breakfast, we headed down to Arvasar where we picked up one of John Mannal's moorings, topped up with water, phoned home to advise we would be late, but would arrive early Saturday morning. Then we were off, joy of joy – no beating, a broad reach down to Eigg, a closer leg to Ardnamurchan then free her off and run down the Sound of Mull.

It fell dark, somewhere of Ardmore Point while the skipper was slaving away in the galley, but the resulting ham risotto went down a treat as we eased sheets and shook out reefs. The crew thoroughly enjoyed every minute of these last miles. We ghosted into Dunstaffnage to lie alongside a pontoon at 04.00 with 286 miles on the clock and a very satisfied skipper and crew – especially as it transpired that most other charter boats had travelled no further than Tobermory.

CIRCUMNAVIGATING THE SHETLANDS

One summer I was invited to skipper a charter boat from Kirkwall in Orkney on a ten day cruise in late July. The charter party had sailed with me before and were keen to visit a few more islands and visit some that we had missed.

The Shetland Isles are the farthest north part of the United Kingdom and lie one hundred miles NNE of the mainland. Separated from Orkney by the Fair Isle Channel, a seventy mile wide stretch of water joining the Atlantic to the North Sea. Fair Isle lies about halfway across the exposed tide-riven strip, much used by super tankers and bulk carriers.

On the other hand, the Orkneys lie close enough to the North Coast to be clearly visible most times. They are separated by the much maligned Pentland Firth with tides up to twelve knots. These seem to be a barrier to many U.K. yachtsmen as most visiting yachts are German, Dutch or Norwegian, which is a pity because the "North Isles", as the locals call them, have much to offer.

We met at Kirkwall on the Wednesday evening, and over a super meal in the Kirkwall Hotel, made some outline plans for the following ten days. This sort of plan needs to be flexible because of the vagaries of the weather. Anyway, we agreed to make an early start by storing-up from the nearest supermarket. One of the crew had driven up, so his car was loaded, and we were ready to take over *Norlantic* (a Moody 346) by midday. I had already checked over the boat, so we were able to stow our gear and food, then set off smartly

Our first call was to be the Island of Rousay, known as Little Egypt of the North, because of it's one hundred plus archaeological sites We intended to use a mini bus tour, then walk along the shore of Eynhallow Sound on the Westness Walk. As Rousay is near Kirkwall, we arrived under three hours, and taking advice from some locals, we tied up on the east side of the Ferry Pier. We arrived to see the mini bus unload the last lot of explorers, and arranged a time.

After tea, we joined the bus and were treated to a running commentary about which beach the Vikings pulled up their longships on, and where the Stone Age Picts kept their shellfish alive. It is a very interesting place, and in no time we were decanted above a footpath stretching down the side of a fairly steep field with a fantastic view of Eynhallow Sound and Island.

At the foot of the paths, we saw a collection of Stone Age brochs, fortified towers and Viking halls. The big attraction was the burial chambers. For protection from the elements it has been covered in by a well-constructed roof, having lots of clear panels to let in light. It is quite long and ship-shaped, with half stone bulkheads to separate the tombs.

Broch exterior and interior

Rousay Ship Burial Chamber

All went well and we arrived back on board for supper and a good rest, for we planned to head of to Fair Isle early on Friday. Crossing the Westray Firth is always an exciting project with its strong tides and "Roosts"(Viking for *races* or *rips*) It is narrow and deep, so there is no real problem, but we wanted to be on the east side as early as possible. We had a fair bit to go if we wanted to be in Fair Isle by evening.

There was a cracking breeze from the Southeast, so we would have a beam reach all the way – about seventy miles. It was a grand morning and the crew, being in a holiday mood, opted for a comfortable breakfast at anchor in the lee of Eday, a green isle with lots of farms, cattle and a nice quiet sandy anchorage.

On the way once again, we decided to pull down the first reef and were soon doing six and half knots flying along towards North Ronaldsay, with its candy striped lighthouse on Dennis Head. When we cleared that, the sea began to get up and the wind was now force-six, so we pulled in the second reef, and still we flew along. What fun.

North Haven Fair Isle

The S.E. wind created a haze, so we didn't see the Fair Isle until it was about four miles on our beam, but as the North Haven is sheltered from southerly winds we headed in close to Skroo Lighthouse, and motored in. It is now joined to the South side and forms part of a new breakwater and pontoon.

The pilot book shows a view from the north where a stack in the harbour entrance comes in line with a deep gully farther south, rather like the sights on a rifle, and takes you right in to a very snug harbour. We tied up alongside a large Norwegian ketch.

Puffins at Fair Isle

As it was late, we ate and celebrated a great start to our trip. Unfortunately, there was no local ceilidh. In the past, they have been great fun, with locals and invited musicians. The next day, after breakfast, we explored, and agreed to meet up for lunch. Fair Isle is really a magic place – we took pictures of Artic Skuas and Puffins, and enjoyed the warm sun while chatting to the islanders. They run a well-stocked community shop. The husband of the post mistress makes excellent spinning wheels for D.I.Y. Fair Isle knitters. He is also a great fiddler and takes part in the weekly ceilidhs. After an alfresco lunch, we headed for Sumburgh Head, keeping a lookout for tankers and bulk carriers. A couple of hours later, we saw the outline of Fitfull Head, the western corner of the mainland of Shetland. It was still a bit hazy and we couldn't see Sumburgh Head. Fitfull is much higher than Sumburgh, so easier to see, and as long as we kept it open to port, we would be okay.

Fitfull is the last resting place of the ill-fated tanker *Braer*, and not a good place to be close to in a storm. However, we were enjoying a great sail with a steady south easterly breeze – fine and sunny as well. As Sumburgh came clear, we noticed large numbers of sea birds, which is usually a good sign of sprats or mackerel.

We headed up the east side of the headland and opened a view of the airport in the entrance to Gruteness Voe. The entrance has a nasty shoal called the "Baas", which is avoided by keeping closer to the north shore. We found a berth on the ferry pier and soon tied up – the tides here have quite a small range. A two metre range is a big spring tide, so tying up is not a problem. A short walk up the road and you can visit The Sumburgh Hotel or "Jarlshoff" – The Vikings "Earls Court" of Shetland. The visitor centre has a fantastic mural depicting Iron and Stone Age settlers, whose homes are all around, and of the Vikings, who followed later. While we are enjoying the scenery, I always like to tell the crew that they are now standing on the 60th parallel of north latitude, the same as Cape Farewell on Greenland.

Back at the pier, we found a visiting motor cruiser from Lerwick that took out sea anglers on a daily basis. The skipper was very helpful and from his chart showed me where to try for ling and cod. It always saves time if you can get some local knowledge.

After dinner, we planned the next few days – hoping to call in at Mousa first, about fifteen miles up the coast, and then on towards to the top of Shetland to visit as many islands as we could. The options are numerous: you can choose to cut through by at least two different gaps between the islands – the Yell Sound or the Blue Mull Sound.

On leaving Sumburgh, we found a fair swell running up from the South East. This was a bit of a mystery as we hadn't heard anything about strong winds in the North Sea. It is not uncommon to get very big swells coming in from the Western Ocean, but not on the east side.

As we approached Mousa, we saw the swell breaking heavily on the rocks and decided not to try for a landing. Instead, we took pictures of the famous Broch, which is ninety percent complete and well worth a visit.

However, we decided to press on and soon entered Lerwick harbour. It is a very sheltered bay, protected from the east by Birsay Island, and crammed with cruise liners, fishing boats and a basin full of yachts. Things were going well and, as we all knew Lerwick well, we kept going through the North entrance, heading for Whalsay. We had been told that they now had a well-laid-out marina as well as a sheltered harbour, so we picked our way through a scatter of small islands and lighthouses, including Symbister and Oot Skerries with its major light in the background.

Approaching the well-marked entrance, we could see several large fishing boats dressed overall, and wondered what was going on. Once inside and tied up to the visitor's pontoon, we soon found out that we had just missed a week's celebration to mark the centenary of the local regatta. Very few people were about, but the yacht club had a huge banner welcoming visitors to the celebration. They must have had a great week – we hardly saw anyone – of course, it was Sunday!

Monday dawned bright and sunny, and we did a bit of shopping and had a shower at the yacht club. Although it is a fairly remote island, it is well-served by hourly ferries from the mainland, and showed signs of early trade with Europe in the shape of a "Hanseatic" Warehouse. We had agreed that now was the time to make a dash for Muckle Flugga, the most northerly lighthouse in Britain. So we set of for Ultima Thule, as the Romans called it, and headed north for Unst and Balta Sound. We went NE inside the group called Out Skerries, and I saw from the chart that we would soon cross a thirty metre bank near Muckle Skerry. As we crossed the bank , it looked a likely spot to catch some fish. I called for a short "heave to" and dropped a line bristling with cod lures bought in Kirkwall. "Knock knock" and up comes a nice ling of about five pounds. Great – guess what we had for dinner !

Soon, we sailed into Balta Sound and tied up alongside. Within easy walking is the hotel, which is the most northerly pub in Great Britain, so we had to visit. The locals thought we were misguided to round Muckle Flugga anti-clockwise, but I'm convinced they just wanted us to stay! Great guys the Shetlanders, they even have their own brewery on Unst. By now the weather had changed, but after a delicious meal, of baked ling and dill sauce, we felt sure the rain wouldn't spoil our trip too much. Fortunately, early morning rain gave way to showers and we set off in high hopes, with everything in our favour. The friendly harbour mistress had provided us with a hose, so we filled our tanks with water before leaving.

The wind was still SSE. We had planned to catch the ebb when up to the NE corner of Unst, called "Holm of Skay", thereby avoiding some nasty roosts. It worked, and as we turned the corner, there was Muckle Flugga – perched on the detached island about four miles ahead. Just shortly after altering course to the west, we crossed another bank, so I thought, *lets see if there are more fish up here,* and, in minutes flat, we had two very plump codling on deck for another feast.

The sun didn't come out for us to sail past Muckle Flugga, but we took some pictures as the tide accelerated us by at an impressive speed. We shot through the gap between the lighthouse and the off-lying stack with at least two knots of tide helping us along. We could see all the coast down to Ramna Stacks at Yell. The sea breeze held and we beam reached down outside at a good seven knots.

" Great, we've done it" This called for a celebration, and all we needed to do now was pick a stopping place for the night. We could either nip into Yell Sound at the Ramna Stacks or keep going for a few miles more to Ronas Voe, which suited us fine – and it looked snug. The approach was rugged with rock stacks and cliffs, but once inside, it was smooth and almost windless, but no pier. So we had to anchor for only the second time this trip.

Once she was secured, we filleted the cod, dipped them in egg and otmeal, and fried up four enormous chunks of the freshest, tastiest fish supper you could wish for. Next morning, we awakened to a surrounding mob of screaming terns hunting for food. As we were about five miles in from the open sea, we decided to eat our breakfast on the way. Once clear of the cliffs at the entrance, we headed west to clear a small island called

"Muckle Ossa". If you haven't already guessed *Muckle* is Scots for *large*.

I hoped for more sea food on a likely bank a little further away. Our luck was out because a land breeze sprang up and formed a mist that very soon became a fog. It was impossible to find the bank without wasting a lot of time. However, as soon as we headed for Pappa Stour, a N.W. breeze sprang up and sped us on our way. We piled on the canvas and were soon making a comfortable six knots as we sped southwards again.

Plan "A" was to head to St Ninian Isle, near the bottom end of the mainland. Plan "B" involved stopping at Foula, the little rocky island twenty miles west of the mainland. We had previously visited both, but Foula had a snug little harbour and some fantastic cliffs so both plans were favourites. We would just have to wait and see!

For those who like verse try Thomas Alexander Robertson, aka Vagaland's poem: *Da Sang o da Papa men*

> Oot bewast da Horn o Papa,
> Rowin Foula doon!
> Owir a hidden piece o water,
> Rowin Foula doon!
> Roond da boat da tide-lumps makkin,
> Sunlicht trowe da cloods is brakkin;
> We maan geng whaar fish is takkin,
> Rowin Foula doon!

After passing Pappa Stour and the Ve Skerries Lighthouse, we could feel the mysterious southerly swell again. As Foula was shrouded by mist, we were happy to head down to St Ninians Isle. The wind held good, and we soon arrived at the entrance to the North harbour called "Bigton Wick" and sailed in to a superb calm bay, with clear water and sandy bottom.

St Ninian's Isle

We anchored as close to the sand bar that joins the isle to the shore as was safe, as we intended to row ashore and explore. The weather had cleared up and it was great, on a lovely sunny evening, to get ashore and stretch our legs. It is a fantastic spot, as no matter what the weather is up to, you can anchor north of the quarter-mile sand bar or south if you prefer. Both sides enjoy complete shelter and are easy of access.

Having used this anchorage several times in the past, I was keen to get some photos from the island that forms the two bays. It is impossible to get the whole picture from onboard, but now we could take our time and explore.

It was well worth it. We disturbed lots of rabbits and were able to look down on the sand splits that joins the island to the mainland. After supper, we made some serious plans, having about seventy miles to get back to Kirkwall, and we did not want to rush it. Everyone was happy to do a night sail, so we left just before dark, at about eleven o'clock, and headed for Westray. The tide would be west-going after midnight.

Bruce and Michael opted for the first three hours watch, and we motored out as planned, but the breeze died, so we kept the engine on to give us five and a half knots, and soon opened up Sumburgh Head Light, which we would be able to see until up on Fair Isle. I often think navigation is easier on a dark night when you have some powerful lights to take bearings from. They are much easier to identify, and this cuts out guess work on bits of land that are barely visible.

We were heading to Eday for good shelter, or Pierowall if that looked a better bet. Soon, we opened up the light on the south end of Fair Isle "Skadan", and a breeze sprang up from the south. We set two-thirds of the Genoa, she steadied up and the speed increased to over six knots. She was now much easier to steer, but the breeze brought drizzle and poor visibility, so we lost the lights. We now relied on GPS or "Nigel the Navigator" as we liked to call it.

The night soon passed, with regular cuppas and watch changes helping. With daylight bringing improved visibility, we saw Mull Head on Pappa Westray dead ahead. This put us about three miles north of our intended track – leeway, I guess. We began to beat down towards the large, sheltered area known as the "North Sound" with Eday at its Southern Corner. While on the port tack, we stand in close to Pappa Westray and see white water ahead – another roost!

With spray flying everywhere, and bang crash wallop we went about and soon returned to calm water and saw the Red Head of Eday ahead. In the early morning sun, the cliffs appeared to be on fire – deep red, just like the Red Head at Lunan Bay. During all the excitement, we hadn't noticed the life-raft forward of the mast had escaped from the lashings and nearly launched it's self, so we slowed down and secured it again.

Our last tack took us back to the anchorage with smooth water and sandy bottom: Freshness Bay. We anchored and devoured helpings of porridge, followed by a long forty winks siesta! We now felt ourselves close enough to Kirkwall, less than twenty miles, so celebrated the trip with a few malts and an early night.

Before heading south, we agreed a second visit to Ork Egilsay, where there is another St. Magnus Church. Apparently, his companions were not so saintly – they ganged up and murdered him there!

We hit the full flood when crossing the Westray Firth, needing to use full throttle as our attempts to counteract the current almost brought us to a stand still! It was so bad that we needed the Genoa to pull us through. The log showed 7.6 knots, but the GPS only gave us 0.8 knots over the ground.

Once clear of that little lot, things began to look up – the sun came out and we tied up to the inside of the inter-isle ferry pier. On deck, in sight of the church, we lunched on sweet, pickled, Orkney herring. We took enough snaps to satisfy the most devout church goer. From the time-tables, we saw that the next ferry was due at 13.30. It was time to head off, on the last of the flood, to make our way back to Kirkwall (using St. Magnus's Catherdal Spire as a leading line) and we tied up alongside in time for an end-of-trip feast ashore.

We had visited eight islands, tied up alongside six, and only anchored twice – with 357 miles logged. The crew had achieved a great deal, and set off home with lots of wonderful memories.

CIRCUMNAVIGATING HARRIS AND LEWIS

Trying to plan a special trip for whole year in advance is a gamble at the best of times, but going round the West Side of the Outer Hebrides calls for settled weather

The crew, Mary and Bob from W. Midlands, John from Cheshire and Bruce from Edinburgh (who had sailed with me on a fair few previous voyages) were all very good, and said they wouldn't mind if it didn't come off. A bit of pottering around and eating ashore would make a change, besides not needing a second holiday to get over the trip.

We stored up *Goldrush*, a Westerly Corsair, for two weeks in Oban — not knowing when we might get to the next shop. So, with plenty of goodies and extra refreshments in case of a heat wave, we set off. The sea breeze boded well for us as we headed up the Sound of Mull to Loch Aline for our first stop.

The forecast was for more S.E. up to force eight on the morrow Thursday. So we planned a quick dash to Loch Drumbuie, up the Sound of Mull, with three reefs in the main and six knots on the clock, and spent a quiet night tasting malts and planning our next move.

Canna is a great place to be with any kind of weather. It is halfway to everywhere and easy access, so that's where we headed for, and made great time. So good that we kept going for Loch Harport and Carbost. The view of the Cuilins, when sitting at the head of the loch, is spectacular. The pub at Carbost is a favourite stop, with excellent pub grub and man-eating midges. We were very snug on a visitors mooring, and the forecast was S.E., but with winds of force seven to eight for the week-end. After another quiet and uneventful night, we wakened to find a sunny morning and the coastguard chirping about gales, so we decided to stay put. We had thought of visiting Tasker Distillery, the main attraction at Carbost, but you can't win them all.

By mid-morning, we had a near gale gusting force eight and our log records "sea smoke"; by mid-day, that's normally force ten. Then we saw this dark-hulled MFV, which had been moored close inshore where I have often anchored, bearing down on us at a steady rate. Either his anchor had dragged or been carried away, but there he was looming larger, with no-one aboard. We started the engine and stood by to slip, hoping he would miss our boat, but no such luck. He was determined to ram us! At 12.06 he was much too close, so we slipped and shot off at better than seven knots under bare pole.

It is funny how you can get so preoccupied with some untoward occurrence. We couldn't remember his name or number, or where he might land, but we were not hanging around to find out. Our main concern was what would it be like at the next stop, about four miles down-wind. Portnalong used to be a favourite stopping place at the entrance to Loch Harport, but recently it has become crowded with fish cages and commercial craft. So I wasn't very happy about our prospects, except it would be smooth water. We were lucky, we nosed in behind some boats and cages, and put the hook down, but of course it failed to bite the first time. The second attempt worked, and after the usual burrowing in the sail locker, we had our kedge out with about thirty metres of chain and warp, and holding fine! Great stuff these evolutions. And there we were: watching others watching us, as they decided what to do. We celebrated in the time honoured manner, which always seems to involve "splicing the main brace" That was followed by an excellent dinner of home-made mushroom soup and beef stew. High living indeed, but before we knew it we were on anchor watch.

My stint was from 00.30 to 05.00. It was a clear, starry night with fewer gusts. By 06.30, we called it off, as it decreased to a strong breeze. So that's how we lost a whole Saturday, safely moored between two anchors, one each bow with about forty degrees between them. All we had to do was tighten up the kedge warp as it stretched. This cuts down the yaw, which otherwise could have the yacht veering about 100 degrees or more – like a kite on a string.

Neist Point Lighthouse

By the time the crew surfaced and had a well-earned breakfast, it was mid-day. We pushed off with a view to eat on the way and make tracks for Rodel at the S.E. entrance to the Sound of Harris. The breeze was southerly and veering, so we had a quick look at McLeod's Maidens and a pleasant sail up past Neist Point. There, the Minch is only twelve miles wide with spectacular cliffs up around Dunvegan Head.

We took bearings of Maddy Mhor (The Big Tooth) at the entrance to Loch Maddy. The wind soon fell and the engine took us to an anchorage in Loch Rodel. We had hoped to use the visitor mooring in the basin off the hotel, but chickened out as it was a falling tide and the channel dries out at 0.9m.

As usual, this meant a somewhat later visit to the pub where we were amazed to find a completely re-built modern bar – the only bar allowed to sell Royal Household Malt – and restaurant, but had forgotten it was Sunday. Last orders were called as we arrived. Oh well, we could have missed out altogether. Next day, Monday, we headed round to Leverburgh and tied up to the pier for water and some additional stores, then off to Taransay of Castaway fame. It's been a favourite shelter when the sea state has indicated that St. Kilda is not a good option, but this time it was our chosen first stop on the West Side, with a view to explore at our leisure.

The long sand pit that juts out halfway to Luss Kintyre makes a super breakwater and seems to be home to numerous seals and seabirds. It also provided us with a great anchorage for another memorable dinner.

Next day we rowed ashore in bright sunlight to explore the island and take pictures. The view from the summit of Ben Raah was superb, with St. Kilda on the Western Horizon looking like a galleon, and Scarp, away to the N.W., and Luss Kintyre Sands spread out across the Sound to the East. As I descended, the outlook got better so I took several photos to try to capture the detail and grandeur of the scene Impossible!

We were now keen to move on to Scarp, which was only eight miles away, and the day was fine. We passed a rugged headland and saw a small craft berthing at a stone pier where some cars were parked. The entire population had just migrated because, when we arrived, it was deserted. Two of the houses were obviously habitable, but the remainder were all derelict. It was a beautiful spot that cried out to be explored, so we made for the shore and were most impressed by the central hill that dominated the whole island. The sands gleamed white, making the shallows of the Sound quite brilliant. The Scarp Sound is so shallow we decided not to risk heading north, but doubled back and circumnavigated clockwise and tucked under Duisker, a small island to the north, before heading up to Ardmhor Mangersta.

Another fine day with a southerly breeze gave us plenty of time to admire the scenery, but, as usual, there wasn't enough time to explore every bay and sea loch, besides, we would find plenty in Loch Roag. We were using the chart that covers The Sound of Harris to Armore Mangersta, and the high mountains were giving way to the rolling hills of Lewis.

We passed Loch Resort, with its entrance sheltered by Scarp; Loch Tealasavay and Tamanavay, with their sheltered anchorages; then outside the small island of Mealasta. From here, it was only six miles to Camus Uig and a welcome break. However, as we rounded in to the bay, we could see that the gentle swell was breaking heavily and providing great sport for surfers. Anchoring was out of the question, as we were rolling like a barrel when we reached ten metres, so we headed back out just after noon, and kept heading north for Gallan Head before anchoring close inshore, in much smoother water, opposite Traigh Na Clibhe.

After a welcome cup of tea, we decided it would be better round the corner at Valtos, so upped anchor and motored round about three miles. This is truly a wonderful spot with a mile of white sand, and some caravans looking out over smooth water, sheltered by medium-size islands. We saw only one other yacht, a small, open Gaffer that was enjoying ideal conditions.

Over supper, we decided that next day, Thursday, we would head back out round Bernera, look for fresh water at Bresclete Pier, and go ashore to explore the standing stones at Callanish. As we motored out, we lost count of the tiny, sandy beaches, and small islands that keep the swell out of East and West Loch Roag. The outermost one is a bit of a landmark called Old Hill, which has deep water all round it. So we passed inside him before heading east towards Loch Carloway, where there is a small harbour and good anchorages. But if we were going to have time at Callanish we must keep going.

At mid-day, we tied up at Bresclete. Many years ago, I unloaded a cargo of coal there and spoke to some fish-farm men who said it was safe to stay as they were leaving and wouldn't be back. The modern factory, which was built to air freeze cod some years ago, now belongs to a pharmaceutical company that employs a fair-sized work force to manufacture drugs. Who would believe it?

While we stretched our legs, a friendly local who was cutting the grass asked where we were from and where we were going. He kindly offered to drive us round to the Standing Stones and told us we could catch a bus back later. This saved us leaving the pier and threading our way through some narrow channels, so we accepted and were soon snapping away like all the other tourists. These stones are remarkable in as much as they are laid out in the form of a Celtic cross – and are virtually intact. When we had enough photos, we repaired to the café for a decent lunch, before catching a west-bound bus, and were soon back aboard.

We had already decided that, as we couldn't visit all the anchorages, the best one for us would be in the Kyles of Little Bernera. This lovely anchorage has a wide eastern entrance and keyhole for a west exit. Once inside it is unbelievably sheltered and offered a quick getaway for us on Friday. As you motor in past several fish cages, you can see a beacon, and you can anchor close into the North shore in a tight little bay. We went ashore keen to get a view and claim another island.

Apparently there are about 1,800 islands around Scotland and I'm still short of 100. It was midge-free and we could see from its summit several more white, sandy beaches and some small islands seaward to seaward. On the other side of the Kyle was a pier, used by the fish-farm workers, which was connected to a road system that could get you to Stornaway via bridges etc. So, although we were really remote, it was an illusion.

Butt of Lewis

After a sumptuous dinner, we sat on deck in the sun and planned a long hop for Friday – round the Butt of Lewis and over to the Summer Isles. It was about 80 miles, which meant an early start for us. We had several debates on whether to carry on round the Top of Lewis, as originally planned (to go all the way up to North Rhona, a smaller version of St Kilda that lies 40 miles north of Lewis) or just retrace our steps to The Sound of Harris. The Butt won! North Rhona has eluded me over the years owing to weather or swell, but now we simply didn't have time.

Friday was almost perfect except for virtually no wind, and we motored out at 07.00 to see if there was a breeze anywhere. No such luck. Anyway, we stood off about three miles in hope, and enjoyed the scenery, with a few dolphins for company. Our log entry for the Butt of Lewis was: 11.45 B.L. Lt House abeam about 1 mile and 25 miles logged. I had previously only seen the Butt in the distance when I was on passage to Cape Wrath, so I can now claim to have "Rounded the Butt".

It was a fine, clear day and we were able to take bearing of Tiumpan Head and Coigeah Nhor, the 5th Big Ben south of Cape Wrath. After a very smooth crossing of the North Minch, we arrived in the sheltered harbour of Tanera Mhor, in the small isles. Bill Wilder, the owner, is a very helpful chap and has a resident engineer who, in the past, has solved some problems for us in his well-equipped workshop. Unfortunately, the Wilders were on the mainland, so we had the place to ourselves. From here on, the voyage was more civilised – with calls at Potree and the Forge Inn at Loch Nevis for a fantastic seafood platter. Then off to Tobermory for music.

We arrived home to Dunstaffnage with 459 miles logged and memories of a great voyage to keep us going for a while.

BUCHAN NESS & THE BULLERS OF BUCHAN

On an early yachting trip, a neighbour had agreed to help deliver my old Gaff Rigged Cutter *Stormalong* to the Moray Firth. We planned a family holiday in this great cruising area, so full of fishing harbours, sandy beaches – and almost fog free.

On the trip from Tayport, we soon ran into strong north-east winds, and thought ourselves lucky to get into Stonehaven.

Before long, the weather improved. I phoned home to find a replacement for my crew, as my friendly neighbour had to leave. Luckily, his substitute was a keen sailor who worked as a Met Officer at Leuchars airfield.

He arrived bright and early the next morning, and we worked out a passage plan. He knew all the Met Boys around the Scottish Coast, so phoned up his chum at Dyce Airfield, and got the all clear. We left right away and found a better picture – with a south-east breeze and reasonable sea. *Stormalong* made good progress up the coast of Aberdeenshire, heading for Buchan Ness at about five knots.

When well past Aberdeen, our radio came alive and spoiled the morning with a cryptic message. "Attention all shipping, new gale warning for sea areas Cromarty and Forth; south-east gale imminent."

Oh well! As we had sight of what looked like Buchan Ness, I was not too worried. We would soon be round the corner and into the harbour of refuge at Peterhead. I couldn't remember how the lighthouse at Buchan Ness looked. Through binoculars, a chimney at the new power station at Boddam, just past Buchan Ness, appeared. It was near enough to give us good bearings and make sure our course would see us pass clear.

When about two miles off, the sea and swell built up, and with a south-east gale on our quarter, the boat flew along like a swallow. We passed quite close to a coastal fishing boat that showed a noticeable roll, lying beam-on to the sea. Our crew felt quite smug as *Stormalong* held her course as steady as a rock, and comfortable with it. As soon as we passed the lighthouse on Boddam Point, the Peterhead Harbour breakwater appeared. The waves breaking over it made for a fearsome sight.

According to the pilot book, the gap in the breakwater (the entrance to the harbour) was eighty-yards wide. From our position, it looked tiny – framed in breaking seas. Aiming for the dead centre of this awesome scene was vital.

I lost no time in deciding we carried too much sail and travelled far too fast, so we dropped the main and proceeded under staysail. That gave us more time to keep her heading for the centre, and in no time at all we broke through into a different world. The sea lay calm, but the inner harbour looked crowded with a fishing boat tied up alongside a pier, halfway to the inner entrance.

The crew of the fishing boat sat on deck sorting out their catch of shrimps. They waved for us to come alongside. We accepted their invitation and the fresh fish rejects from their catch. As it was near lunch time, the crew opened a bottle of whisky to celebrate our arrival.

KINNAIRD HEAD LIGHTHOUSE

Kinnaird Head was the first lighthouse purpose-built by the newly formed Northern Lighthouse Board, and is unique. In 1787, they chose a site on the headland that juts into the North Sea (just beyond the entrance to Fraserburgh Harbour) but it included an ancient castle.

Sir Walter Scott, one of the board members, objected strongly to knocking a historic building down for the benefit of a new light-tower. As a compromise, they built the tower inside the castle wall. It stood high enough to give the light the best visibility from the Moray Firth's shore, out to sea, and down the coast towards Rattray Head – a huge coverage. It is now a NLHB visitor centre and shop.

Seeing this lighthouse for the first time proved memorable. I had agreed to deliver a home-completed thirty-six-foot steel-hulled motor-sailor called *Sanda*. She had spent most of the winter in Anstruther, drying out on every tide, and her compass was well out – due to banging against the harbour wall twice a day.

I had agreed to swing her compass on the river Tay, and we looked after her for a couple of weeks while making some changes to the keel. The owner brought an ex-seafarer friend, and I brought a former pupil (newly qualified as a Yacht Master). We planned to leave early afternoon. This coincided with High Water, which would give us a favourable ebb, heading north for seven hours.

As luck would have it, the weather closed in and dense fog wrapped itself around us. *Sanda* made about seven knots under engine, but had no radar or electronic navigation aids, so it was dead reckoning all the way. However, I had bought the latest hand-held Radio Direction Finder, to help my students at the winter RYA evening classes, and had it with me.

As we approached Inverbervie, I knew the water was deep, and free from rocks, so wasn't too worried on hearing lots of seagull noise. The cliffs to the north of the village rise about 60ft, and the water is around the same depth. So I fixed our position, and altered out to head for Buchan Ness. There we experienced the usual heavy swell, and I concluded our "dead reckoning" was okay – that meant the compass was spot on. As daylight crept in, I managed to fix a steady bearing on Kinnaird Head Lighthouse's RDF Beacon – sounding "KD" in Morse code. It was about thirty degrees on our port bow, and I felt reassured as it fitted in nicely.

The owner had a sceptical opinion of this piece of equipment, and wasted no time saying so. However, we opened bearings at a steady pace as it came abeam (right angles to our heading). I called to the owner to switch on the echo sounder. This showed deep water below us (some 30-odd metres) and I altered course to bring the bearing dead ahead. As the signal strengthened, I asked the owner to slow down to about half speed.

Bit by bit, the depth reduced to 10 metres, and what should appear out of the fog but the majestic castle and tower of Kinnaird Head Lighthouse, soaring above us. Talk about pulling white rabbits out a hat! The owner appeared dumbfounded, but looked as happy as I felt. We altered course to head up the Firth to Inverness. In less than a mile, the fog disappeared and the Moray Coast lived up to its nickname: *The Riviera of the North.*

Kinnaird Castle Lighthouse, from an 1822 print by William Daniell

NEW HORIZONS

Hyskeir (OIGH Sgeir" Fl (3) 30s 41m 24M

56° 58·2'N 06° 40·9'W

Hyskeir Light stands on the smallest of the Small Isles, south of Canna and west of Rhum. This major light, covers the Sea of the Hebrides and Approaches to The Minch. When still manned, it had a non-directional radio beacon fitted, with a call sign in Morse code: OR. During my time as Principal RYA Instructor for Hebridean Cruising (based at Dunstaffnage) I was often glad of the radio beacon. It helped to show budding Yacht Masters how to find the channel between Oigh Sgeir and the buoy marking the Humla Rock, about two miles north.

When homeward-bound from Loch Boisdale, in poor visibility, the radio beacon allowed us to do a running fix. This, used along with soundings, would put us between the buoy and the light. I often wondered about landing there, but was usually put off by large breakers on its reef.

Then, one day, I received an excited call from my youngest daughter Wendy: "Dad! You'll never guess where I'm working – the head office of the Northern Lighthouse Board in Edinburgh!"

Well, I thought, *here is an opportunity not to miss.* "Great," I said, "see if you can get me a drawing of the harbour at Hyskeir" – and she did. Not long after, I had a sketch and a note, from Captain MacFarlane, Superintendent of N.L.H.B.

The plan and notes rattled around in my sea-going briefcase for several years, waiting for a suitable occasion to make a landing. It took its time. When I was in the area, the swell and white breakers seemed to warn off any approach, until one trip. While heading north – bound for Canna, halfway up the west side of Rhum – the light south-west breeze died away.

There we sat, "a painted ship upon a painted ocean" with a glassy-calm sea reflecting the Rhum Cuilins to our east and the low-lying island of Hyskeir to the west. At last, we had ideal conditions to explore some new islands. So it was on with the engine and alter course for the south entrance to the anchorage, about five miles west.

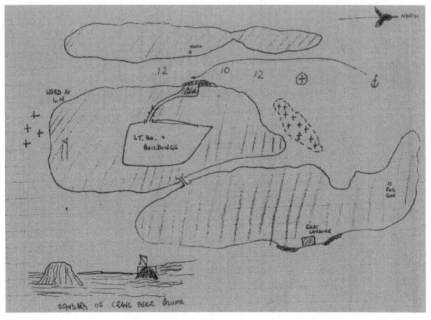

Captain MacFarlane's Sketch

The note from Captain MacFarlane explained: "When approaching from the south" (as we intended) "keep the crane on the jetty centred on a Black Bluff to its south, then alter straight into the channel". This was soon done and the small crane hove into view. As *Stormalong* turned towards the pier, she floated swan-like over the white sand – now reflecting the warm sun from the sea floor. We slowed down as the reefs on each side appeared to close in, but the bottom looked clean and the water too deep for an anchor. At the pier, we spoke to the three keepers, all fishing for mackerel while enjoying the sun.

Hyskeir Lighthouse

They told us the water wasn't as deep a littler further in, so we proceeded with caution, and on finding eight metres, anchored. Tying up to the pier would have spoiled the keepers' fishing.

We blew up the inflatable dinghy and rowed back to explore our latest island. The keepers seemed very pleased to see us, and showed their goodwill with a conducted tour of the light. It is an imposing structure – all white with a yellow lantern and a black roof. The light shows on the chart as being forty-one metres above Mean High Water Springs. I remember counting 138 steps, while following one of the keepers to the top.

What a view unfolded from the lantern room. I had never imagined what a difference looking from such a height made. From our usual level of about two metres height-of-eye, only Ardnamurchan Point was visible to the south and west. Now, peeping above the horizon, a small bit of the three peaks on South Uist – the highest being Hecla. So, imagine my surprise when I saw a chain of islands: Coll, Tiree, Barra Head, Berneray, Mingualay, Pabay, Sandray, Vatersay, Barra, Eriskay, and South Uist.

It felt like standing at the centre of a giant lagoon, surrounded by a necklace of distant islands. The view stunned me so much that I forgot to capture it on film. Sadly, the keepers were the last to enjoy their own six-hole golf course and netted-over vegetable plot, as work was already in hand to convert the light to automatic. However, it solved one problem – in prolonged spells of bad weather, they sometimes had to wait months for the relief boat!

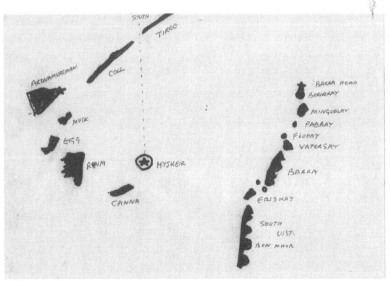

Skerryvore Lighthouse

More recently, when correcting charts of the West Coast, I've had the sad task of "deleting" the foghorn from three of our Rock Lights: Skerryvore, Hysgeir and Ardnamurchan. In foggy weather it was a real comfort to hear their sonorous note bellow out to warn us of doom!

Supper

The perks of sailing

PASSAGE PLANS FOR THE NORTH ISLES

Part One

Having spent many happy days sailing among the Orkney and Shetland Islands, I couldn't help noticing a lack of yachts flying the Red Duster. Dutch, Norwegian, and less often German, passed, but hardly ever a West Coast Yacht. I asked around, and discovered that Cape Wrath proved too much for most of the chaps trying it.

Well, Cape Wrath has a reputation, but like all our main turning points, also plenty of cosy little hideaways where it is safe to anchor and spend some time ashore. I soon discovered the difficulties of making a round trip from Oban to the Orkneys in a single week. What I quickly found out was to start the voyage from Kyle of Lochalsh, or better still, Ullapool – both have plenty of good shops and ample long-term car parking.

Something else I learned from a local – the early part of the summer is often spoiled by fog. The locals never planned regattas, or such, till after the longest day – and they were right, of course. That is not a hard and fast rule, as fog can arise at any time, but generally it works. So, even when we had everything well organised, we still needed to pop into one of our hidey holes to await an improvement.

One of our favourites, Loch Ned, lies between Stoer Point and Kylescu Bridge – very snug, and an easy walk to Drumbeg Hotel. It was so secure that one chap left his yacht there on a single anchor! But if you needed fuel, Loch Inver had that, plus shops and pontoons – and the diesel cost much less.

Once past Loch Ned, you will find one last port with all the necessities – Kinloch Bervie – it has pontoons, but not as many fishing boats as in the past. Not so long ago, around seventy boats worked out of there – and yachts were not welcome.

On one occasion on our way to Cape Wrath, we had it timed for rounding by early afternoon. When a few miles south, a white wall of fog rolled down in our direction. As luck would have it, our position was almost abeam of a great little cove – Sheigra – and we made haste to duck in and anchor, as the fog reached us.

Many years before, while holidaying with the family at Sheigra, a large fishing boat came in to give the crew a break. She had a full shot of monk fish, and gave us a box of beautiful haddock to handout to the campers. The skipper pressed me not to tell anybody where he was hiding, which I did, and I still enjoy the memory.

Once the fog lifted, we got under way, and soon had a great view of the distant Cape Wrath and its lighthouse.

When we cleared the rocky skerries, which guard Sheigra's sheltered cove, we could see the small islet of Ambalg – lying off the southern end of Sandwood Bay. This magical spot, without road or dwelling, is the reputed haunt of mermaids – well, we never did see any, but you never know!

How you round the massive headland of Cape Wrath all depends on the weather and conditions. On a flat calm, it is possible to keep close inshore and pass between the cliffs (where the water is deep) and the Duslic Rock. This lies a mile off the lighthouse, and dries and breaks heavily in any sea. But in a blow, or if it is going to be a beat, then keep about five miles off – where you miss the back scatter of the seas bouncing off the cliffs.

Once round the corner, it will depend on the circumstances: either head up to the entrance of Hoy Sound and Stromness, or chose a well-earned break in Loch Eribol. The imposing mass of Whiten Head, at the east side of the entrance, marks this well-sheltered sea loch. If a short stay is your aim, Rispond Bay (just inside the western entrance after passing three Isles to starboard) has good holding and shelter from westerly's. Anchor in sight of a stone-built drying harbour.

However, halfway along the east shore lies the small island of Ardneackie (joined to the shore by a shingle bank) where a long stay would be more comfortable.

From Loch Eribol to Orkney can prove fairly straight forward, depending on the weather. Given a sea breeze, a broad reach will take you up to Hoy Sound, which is the short route to Stromness. This is a fantastic mark for sea anglers and often yields large cod and ling. The Hoy Sound is well-marked by Hoy High Light. In transit with Hoy Low, it makes the entrance a straight forward night exercise, and there are more lights all the way to the Marina.

Hoy Low Lighthouse

In the event of a disturbed weather pattern, this allows time to explore the Mainland and still duck out the southern entrance to Scapa Flow. In more settled conditions, it's a good scheme to head up to Brough Head. Then either slip into Eynhallow Sound and visit Rousay (more of this later) or press on to Noup Head at the westerly corner of Westray – where several choices await.

Be aware of the North Shoal (unmarked) and lying about twelve miles off Brough Head, with around six feet of water over it. This is a fantastic mark for sea anglers, and often yields large cod and ling. You can either, catch the flood tide down the Westray Firth "strong stuff", or keep on to Papa Westray, and find the way down to Pierowall.

This is a great place to get ashore. It even has its own bakery, sending supplies to half a dozen islands. From here it is possible to visit all twenty-seven islands that make up Orkney, or choose your favourites. Stromness has a lot going for it, including a new marina. Both Capt. Bligh and Capt. Cook stored their ships for the north-west Passage there.

It is also a good centre to visit a whole range of sites from – including Scara Brae and Maes Howe – either by organised tours, or car hire. Most of the islands are well-served by ferry from Kirkwall and Stromness. It is often possible to tie up at the opposite side of the ferry pier to make a good start at exploring.

One island in particular is a must: Rousay. Known as "Little Egypt" it has over 100 archaeological sites. Many are well-preserved, including a massive "ship burial chamber" with a roof over it. A walkway allows a brilliant view down into the partition.

PASSAGE PLAN NORTH ISLES

Part Two

Having arrived in the Orkney Islands, much will depend on the weather. For instance, after a prolonged spell of south-westerlies, a large swell makes itself felt all along the West Coast of the group.

If your arrival port was Stromness, a good plan is to spend a day or two exploring the Stone Village of "Skara Brae" at the Bay of Skaill. This fascinating settlement last rang to the voices of its inhabitants about 3,500 years ago. Violent storms buried it in wind-blown sand, and the buildings did not reappear till the 1800s, when another powerful storm blew the sand out. A wise landowner saw the value of keeping it intact, and prevented the locals from putting the stones to other uses.

Looking down into an empty, roofless house, it is possible to see stone dressers and a fireplace. You can easily imagine the comfort and security the Stone Age tribes enjoyed

Within a radius of about twelve miles from Stromness, it is possible to visit Skara Brae, Maes Howe (a chambered tomb with runic symbols to decipher) and the Standing stones at Steness. All these on the same day, when travelling from Stromness.

A good scheme is to head south to Scapa Flow and pay a visit to the old naval base at Lyness on Hoy. Preserved here are the giant pumps used by the navy to fuel warships lying in the Flow. They also run a continuous film display. Scapa Flow is a diver's paradise, and about a dozen boats visit daily from Stromness – to check out the remains of the German fleet, scuttled on the orders of Rear-Admiral Ludwig von Reuter in 1919.

To the south of Scapa is a huge oil terminal on "Flotta" with its landmark "flare off" noticeable for miles, even in poor visibility. From the middle of the "Flow" it's not far to St Margaret's Hope on South Ronaldsay – the Orkney terminal for the shortest ferry crossing. The Pentland Ferries now use a Catamaran to whisk you across the Pentland Firth. It takes an hour from Gills Bay to St. Margaret's Hope, where there is good shelter and an excellent food eatery.

If the plan is to press on, head south through the Sound of Hoxa (under the massive World War II gun emplacements) past Widewall Bay, and out into the dreaded Pentland Firth. Make sure the tide is with you, and head east between the Pentland Skerries and South Ronaldsay. This way is free from the Atlantic swell, because it is now the North Sea.

From here, it's about fifteen miles to Holm Sound, where the U-Boat crept through on a dark night and sank the "Royal Oak". This led to the plugging (with sunken block ships and Churchill Barriers) of all the narrow gaps. Here you can find a temporary stop that gives good shelter, except from the east. If the bright lights beckon, keep heading north for Deerness and Mull Head, before heading west through Shapinsay Sound and

The String. This is a very narrow passage between Carness and Helliar Holm. Watch out for cruise liners and North Link Ferries tying up at Hatston terminal – opposite Kirkwall Harbour and Marina.

Kirkwall has a new Marina with ninety-five berths, and showers at the sailing club. There are also plenty of good shops and eateries to tempt you to stay. St Magnus Cathedral is central to the town, and is well worth a visit – its mighty spire is visible from Scapa Flow, and for miles northward.

Once the crew check off all the attractions, I recommend a visit to Rousay. A mini-bus leaves from the ferry pier, and will wheel you around to the start of "Westness Walk". This is along the Eyn Hallow Sound, heading east. There are many brochs and burial chambers to visit, and at the end, an inn to relax in while awaiting the mini-bus.

A more sheltered stop is Pierowall (on Westray) where shops and great food are all close to the harbour. There is another "St Magnus" church on the island of Egilsay where, according to Viking legend, one of his close relatives murdered the saint. While ashore at Pierowall you can see where they make the straw-backed Orkney chairs, almost next door to the hotel. Their bar menu includes fantastic fish suppers and an excellent dram called "Scapa" – one of Orkney's best kept secrets.

A short walk from the hotel, stands an interesting ruin – Noltlands Castle. A wealthy local, worried about the threat of Napoleon Bonaparte invading Orkney, built it for his own defence. He wasted his time and money, for it was never needed!

Having slipped past Shapinsay, Stronsay, and Eday, to get nearer to the north of the islands. These can be visited on the return journey home.

From Pierowall, the plan is to head out into the North Sound and steer for North Ronaldsay, through about twenty miles of clear water. This means leaving Papa Westray (which has the record for the shortest air flight) close abeam to port. We now head up to round Dennis Head, with its red and white lighthouse, at the north end of North Ronaldsay. This is because there is a good anchorage just round the head land, with easy access to the road.

The island is unique in having a sea wall all around to keep the cattle on the grass, and the sheep on the shore. There they eat seaweed, which makes for a wonderful-tasting mutton – available in all the Orkney butchers and well worth knowing about.

The anchorage is over-looked by two light-towers – the new red and white one, and a much older stone version that has survived for a long time. On my first visit, we received an invitation from a keeper newly arrived from Oban, to climb up inside the new lighthouse. We looked down on a huge reef that had a brand new wreck sitting upright at its centre. It had been homeward bound for Denmark, with a full shot of fish, and was using modern sails to cut down the high cost of fuel. It seems the crew fell asleep. The lighthouse keeper tried to waken them by firing maroons, but to no avail.

Our anchorage, at the top of Linklett Bay, now placed us to sail off to the Fair Isle – about halfway to Shetland, or twenty-five nautical miles. The Fair Isles channel is twice that width, and much used by large tankers, so keep a good look out!

PASSAGE PLANS

Part 3

Part of the plan for Shetland should include a visit to Fair Isle – famous for it's brightly coloured knitwear. Quite apart from a very sheltered anchorage and pier at North Haven, the islanders run a well-stocked shop. Their fantastic ceilidhs and dances take place in the village hall at weekends.

So, before leaving North Ronaldsay, plan to carry the north-west going ebb, and aim to leave Fair Isle on the port bow. If the weather is kind, and visibility good, as the prominent hill of Sheep Craig draws abeam, it's advisable to close up to within one mile. Once past the cliffs of North Gavel, the Fair Isle North Lighthouse will come into view, so turn in and slow down. North Haven will open up to port, and when the small stack in the mid Channel comes into line with the deep gully below Sheep Craig (almost like a rifle sight) head in, and if lucky, find a new pontoon – or anchor.

Fair Isle South

Fair Isle is a bird-watcher's paradise where many species rest on their south migration. There is also a large resident population of sea birds, including Puffins and Bonxies. The hillside overlooking the haven is an ideal place to get close to puffins. They nest in disused rabbit burrows (flying straight in) but sit outside before taking off. It's quite easy to sit quietly and snap them as they emerge.

Puffins Galore

Up Close

More Puffins

If the weather remains settled, you can plan to continue to Sumburgh Head and along the East Coast of Shetland. But it's just as easy to choose the West Coast, if the weather suits.

If time allows, there is plenty to see going either way. If time presses, I would recommend the East Coast and a visit to

Grutness Voe – just north of Sumburgh Head. This is the sheltered port used by the Fair Isle ferry *Good Shepherd*" Take an easy walk to the Sumburgh Hotel and the Viking site at "Jarslshor" i.e. "Earls Court" – where there are ruins worth a visit.

Heading on up the coast towards Lerwick, you find the Isle of Mousa — it has an nearly complete broch. The entrance to this ancient building is very tight. It could be blocked from a small chamber – sealing it off and protecting the inhabitants from danger. The inside wall has well-built steps leading to the top, and sockets in the inner walls support beams and a roof of skins. This is the best specimen of broch in the U.K still surviving..

From Mousa to Lerwick is fairly straight forward. On entering the harbour, head for Victoria Pier. An assistant harbour master will sort out your berthing needs. Besides getting a berth, a key is available for the sailing club – allowing access to showers, washing machines, and a fine bar. There is also a good supply of shops for all your needs.

Fifteen minutes walk from the harbour, lies the most remarkable and ancient site of "Clickimin". It is well worth the effort. What makes it so different is you can walk on stepping-stones to a small island in a man-made lagoon. There you stand, surrounded by modern buildings, cars, and a busy suburb, but can still inspect a 3,500-years-old broch and wheel house.

The ancient peoples left the island littered with querns, for grinding corn, and they used the tidal lagoon for storing shellfish. If the plan is to circumnavigate Shetland, and the vessel is now stored for the next week, I can recommend heading up for Whalsay. This small island is a bustling fishing port that boasts five millionaires in its fleet.

The harbour at Symbister is easy to spot because of its high stone breakwater. Once inside, there are plenty of berths, including twenty for visitors – unless it's a regatta week. Worth a visit also is the Hanseatic Museums – a small building overlooking the harbour – with examples of German trade goods dating back to 1750. The boating club is open most evenings for showers and the bar.

When quitting Whalsay to head north, leave Out Skerries to starboard and head up for Balta Sound on Unst. This is a very sheltered harbour, getting its name from Balta Island, which lies across the entrance to the sound. Inside the harbour is a pontoon with a fresh-water hose, and a most helpful harbour master is available if you need fuel.

A few minutes walk up the road takes you to the Balta Sound hotel and restaurant – the most northerly hotel in Britain, and well worth a visit. It is now about ten miles to the northern most lighthouse – Muckle Flugga. Getting the tides right is important, as they can run up to over three knots at springs. By leaving shortly before H.W., it is possible to stop and fish just before reaching the top. Using local knowledge, it is best to fish in water a bit deeper than thirty metres (to avoid huge numbers of cuddies) and you have a good chance of pulling up some prime cod and ling!

Muckle Flugga

Muckle Flugga

Once round the top, it is possible to cut back through the Yell Sound and down to Lerwick, or, if the weather is kind, head south for Scaloway. If that's too much of a rush, there are plenty of sheltered Voes to anchor in. My favourite is Ronas Voe, but there are no shore-side facilities there. Farther south, round Eshaness, head in for Muckle Roe Island, and enter Swarbacks Minn – all deep water overlooked by massive naval guns (abandoned after one of the world wars).

Now head north for Busta Voe and the sailing club at Brae. The club doesn't appear to have large numbers of keel boats, but loads of dinghies. It is a fair size, with slips running out from a spacious workshop full of dinghies. Upstairs has a monster of a lounge bar. Brae is an urban development on a narrow isthmus, a stone's throw from the bottom corner of Sulum Voe. From here on, we find a host of choices.

In calm weather, Papa Stour is well worth a visit to see the modern sector-light. This is so powerful you can see it in daylight. From there, it's about twelve miles to Foula – with a modern harbour, and 1,000-foot cliffs thronged with myriads of sea birds.

If the bright lights beckon, aim to visit Scalloway. From here it's about five miles by bus to Lerwick. The boating club there has all the facilities, plus a fantastic restaurant overlooking the berth. De Haaf is a must! Scalloway has plenty of shops and boatyard facilities. A great natural anchorage, called Saint Ninian's Isle, lies about eight miles from Scalloway.

This holy isle is about one mile from north to south, and lies about a quarter of a mile off the south mainland at Bigton Wick. The island joins to the shore by way of a broad sandbank, which seldom covers. It provides great shelter on either side, depending on the wind direction.

Departing from here to head south to Pierowall can be a great night passage, as the Fair Isle Channel is lit up like Piccadily Circus. When you clear Fitfull Head, and come abeam of Sumburgh Head, it might surprise you to know you are on the same latitude as Cape Farewell, Greenland!

Happy sailing, and enjoy the long daylight hours – and the friendly folk.

Time for Tea

Bill and Crew at Tobermory Bay

Studying Chartwork

TOD HEAD

On an early delivery trip – with my number one son Andy – we wanted to get our old gaff Cutter *Stormalong* up to the Moray Firth for the start of our family cruise. Having left Tayport harbour in north-east Fife (opposite Dundee) the previous evening, we had carried the ebb as far as Gourdon, with a fine so'west breeze.

However, as we came abeam of the Minor Light at Tod Head, our wind veered round to nor'-nor'-west, slowing us to a halt. I reckoned our position as not too far from Stonehaven, so it was on with the engine and harden up the main sheet. Even taking in the jib didn't seem to make a lot of difference, and the sea was getting up. To try to improve our situation, I headed closer inshore (we were about two miles off) and our speed began to improve.

Then a one-man lobster boat appeared, coming down wind from Stonehaven. He rounded up on our port side and hailed us to see if we were okay. I replied that we could do with a pluck in to Stonehaven, and he agreed. All the fuss and shouting brought Andy on deck, so I asked him to go forward and stand by the mast. Meanwhile, our friendly lobster-man coiled up a heavy polypropylene tow rope.

I told Andy not to attempt any fancy knots – just catch it and wrap it round the mast at deck level. An excellent throw by the fisherman, and Andy had no problem securing the line. I left the helm, nipping forward to secure the tow to our knight heads (which held the bowsprit steady). *Now we should be okay,* I thought, but not for long. The fisherman shouted over that we were towing him! He couldn't get ahead of us – so we hadn't stopped! Andy ran forward and cast him off while I slowed down a touch, to let him get ahead. He shouted over that he would lead us in.

Sure enough, with his ample beam and power, he smoothed the waves, and we could follow his wake. Talk about "oil on troubled waters"!

Anyway, in time, we gained sight of the harbour breakwater, and soon tied up alongside. The lobster-man returned later, but wouldn't hear of payment, though he accepted a couple of drams. He gave me an excellent tip about keeping close, in bad weather, when approaching from the south: "Keep at least three chimneys on Dunottar Castle in sight, and you will be okay."

Dunottar Castle sits on the edge of massive cliffs just south of Stonehaven, and is a great landmark. When I asked him about the sudden wind shift off Tod Head, he smiled, "That often happens there – it's where the Caledonian fault enters the seas and upsets the weather."

So now I know!

TRUE FROM SEAWARD

A Mariner's View Of Lighthouses

The waters surrounding our British coast are among the most dangerous in the world. Rocks, wrecks, shoals, reefs, and sandbanks – with strong tides running around them – test a navigator's skills to the limit. Add the changeable nature of our coastal weather, and the result can prove deadly.

To a homeward-bound mariner, this adds to the problems of his job. In the open sea, he manoeuvred his ship in hundreds of square miles of sea room, with several thousand metres of water beneath the hull. Inshore, it gets tricky.

One ally in the navigator's struggle to keep his vessel in safe waters, and his feet dry, is the reliability of our lighthouses. In all weathers, when everything else fails, they shine out clear and certain – showing us the way to our chosen haven.

I often say that making a landfall is easier in the dark, because you can identify each light from its characteristic flashes. In daytime, it is difficult to recognize an island, cliff, or headland if the visibility is not perfect.

Of course, navigation is not always easy. One incident stands out as a warning for the unwary. We entered the Southern

Approaches to the Irish Sea, homeward-bound from South America in late December, heading for the Mersey. Our ship was the Royal Mails Line's *Valantia* (formerly a US Liberty ship *Sam Faithful*) with a cargo of corn for breakfast cereals.

We never saw the Bishop Light on the Scillies, and relied on dead reckoning as the ship passed up the Welsh coast. Our turning point was off Anglesey Island, and we needed to see the Skerries Light. This powerful beam has a nominal range of twenty-two nautical miles. The other lights further south – Bardsey or South Stacks – hadn't been seen either, but that was put down to being too far offshore.

The moonlight sparkled on the snow-covered Mount Snowdon. Although dressed like Eskimos, the thinning of our blood from a sojourn in the Tropics, made us shiver in the bitter weather. At last, with our distance run, we saw a light – but it shone blood-red.

A pretty pickle indeed! Our chart made no mention of red, but everything else seemed right. So, helm over to alter course and pass five miles north of Anglesey. That would take *Valencia* up to the Bar Lightship and the Liverpool Pilot Cutter.

As the distance between us and the light shortened, our eyes rounded in amazement at an orange glow now showing. What next? We scratched our heads in disbelief – neither I nor our grizzled skipper had seen the like. At six or seven miles, the colour altered again, to its regulation white.

Lightship

The Old Man banged his fist on the rail. "Of course," he said, "the frost broke up the light – as if shining through a prism!"

With genuine warmth, we welcomed the pilot aboard to complete the voyage to Liverpool.

Typical Liberty ship. Mass produced in USA during the war

TEXAS OR BUST – (BY BOAT):

How I Helped a Demobbed WWII U.S. Air Force Pilot Sail his Yacht Home from Scotland

Stars and Stripes cross the Atlantic

On a recent visit to Tayport, my hometown in Fife, I took a walk to the harbour. And was pleasantly surprised to see it full of yachts on pontoons. Several boats stood along the north wall with owners working on them – and I met some of my former pupils and old chums.

Deep in thought, I wandered around the scene of my youthful haunts. Memories flooded back, especially of an adventurous transatlantic trip I undertook in the company of a US Air Force pilot officer.

The Bell Rock Tavern is still much in evidence. When I first used it before our Atlantic crossing, we called it the "Tide Watchers HQ". Frequent arguments raged among its patrons on whether the sea was coming in or going out.

I was a second mate on an Ex-Liberty Ship, owned by the Royal Mail Line, and had recently acquired a brand new BSA Bantam motorbike. My brother George persuaded me to whiz down to Tayport Harbour to meet an American, John P. Noble, (Jack) who lived aboard *Oregon* – a thirty-foot Falmouth Quay Punt. He had bought the boat the previous year, in the Firth of Forth. When he met the artist Colin Grierson, he moved to Tayport to take advantage of the very competitive harbour dues.

From my first glance down at her deck, it seemed obvious this was a sound seagoing vessel. Cutter-rigged, with a protruding ten-foot bowsprit, *Oregon* was a conventional quay punt of the type built in Falmouth in 1912. The beam of 9 foot by 6 inches was Victorian, to my way of thinking, and unsuited for a long cruise. She carried a great deal of iron ballast (about 4 1/2 tons) and rolled more than necessary.

We climbed down and boarded *Oregon* to meet her owner, who dreamed of sailing his new yacht back to Texas.

After demob in Edinburgh, he had studied medicine at the Royal College of Surgeons where he made friends with some members of the Royal Forth Yacht Club. One thing led to another. He found *Oregon* and decided it would be a great way to travel back to his home in the USA.

Keen to get involved in the war, he had joined the Canadian Air Force and then became a pilot in the Royal Air Force before transferring to the American Air Force. All he knew about navigation was how to "vector" so many degrees – as given by his navigator or controller. He had the wisdom to sign up for a Yacht Master Course at the old Dundee School of Navigation in Bell Street.

When I met Jack, I still had three months sea time before sitting my First Mates Certificate. I already held a Second Mates Certificate and sailed at that rank, so I planned to do one more trip. I would pay off towards the end of March and sign up at Dundee for a three-month course. During that period, John and I made weekend trips to the Forth, and I started to learn a very different style of navigation.

While studying for my next "ticket", I learned it was common practice for ship owners to supply crews with drinking water at the rate of one gallon per day, for voyages abroad. *Oregon* had a twenty-five-gallon galvanised steel water tank, but a Transatlantic voyage would need a lot more. We found two forty-gallon petrol tanks at a local scrapyard in Dundee. The local plumber, Wallace Hughes, adapted them to carry drinking water, and fitted small, brass, drainage taps.

With no facilities for steaming, Jack and I took the tanks to the old harbour and filled them with sea water. They remained tethered to the foot of a ladder for a couple of days before we took them to the plumber. Because of the size and shape, they had to stand vertically each side of the mast – which the boatbuilders had stepped on the keel. That made them secure and easy to fill and use, with little chance of movement and damage.

While travelling around Europe, Jack had met a Londoner called Peter. He asked his friend to join us towards the end of

July, as we hoped to leave Tayport on a big tide. My older brother George arranged to take his summer holiday fortnight, so he could come at least as far as France.

So, after a farewell dinner, we made ready to set sail at High Water on Saturday 29th July 1950... and we did. Our attempts to get extra rations via the Customs failed – they said our requirements didn't fit with their rules – so we bought enough in a local shop to get us to France, for the grand total of £9-18-8p.

Once clear of the River Tay's shallow entrance, we had to beat against a southeasterly breeze. Progress was sea-slug slow. However, noon on Sunday found us off Barnes Ness, but on looking for lunch, we discovered our quota of fresh meat stank. It had to go overboard to feed the fishes. How we wished we had eaten it sooner.

Navigation was almost entirely by the log, though, off Berwick, I managed to get a good fix. I saw a long, well-lit train disappear into a tunnel then reappear just outside the lights of the town. This gave me a V.G. (very good) fix, and we tacked out to seaward. One of our Primus stoves needed a spare part, so we headed into Holy Island to search.

Once ashore, we found plenty of beer, but no spares, so took off for Seahouses – a busy fishing port. I bought a huge sowester, like the ones used by the R.N.L.I., a small galvanised bucket, and 100 hooks – which all came in handy later. From Seahouses we had to beat all the way to Flambourgh Head, and arrived off this well-lit headland on Wednesday evening.

Here our luck changed, and we set full Main and Genoa to a northerly breeze – now we flew – and in the right direction. We carried this sail until 06.00 when our first milestone hove into view– the Dowsing Lightship. At this point, I called all hands to shorten sail. The northerly wind had increased, making the steering harder. We also streamed two mooring warps, one on each quarter, and this helped to keep her from trying to luff up.

We could hand the main together and still keep up a good speed.

When near to the Dowsing Lightship, we hailed her for news of any gale warnings out, but they said no. *Oregon* sailed on towards the next tricky bit.

The Haisborgh Gat is a buoyed channel between the Norfolk Coast and a nasty sandbank of that name. I particularly remember that night because counting the flashes from the buoys proved awkward. They would disappear in the troughs, so it took several attempts to check each one. By the time daylight crept in, we had reached the lee of the land off Lowestoft.

Peter found himself hauled out of his bunk, as the three watch keepers had slept little. While we slumbered, Peter steered on his own till midday. This resulted in some confusion – nobody had kept our position up to date on the chart. Jack climbed aloft and reported seeing a lightship ahead. He bet me it was the "Galloper". I took soundings with the lead line and decided, as it was high tide, we were over the Long Sand. From this chart, I reckoned we were in sight of the Kentish Knoch, and thus became the proud possessor of the last tomato – in settlement of the bet.

We spent the rest of the day tacking down towards the Goodwins, and by noon the next day had almost reached the North Goodwin Light Vessel. Jack started the engine and headed for Calais, the nearest refuge where the crew could rest.

After about four hours motoring, we reached Calais at 21.00, Saturday 5th August, and wasted no time dashing ashore to sample the wine and food. The French cuisine proved excellent plus, owing to postwar problems, we got 1,000 Francs to the £1. A glass of *vin blanc* was 11 Francs – not bad.

We enjoyed a memorable night ashore – with music and dancing in the streets – so we were not alone in celebrating. Next morning, Peter told us the sea didn't agree with him, so he intended to bid farewell and hitch across Europe to Turkey. My brother George still had a week left of his holiday, and hoped to see a lot more of the French Coast. We made for *Le Havre,* where he got a ferry across *La Manche* i.e. the English Channel.

With about 125 miles sailing ahead, we topped up with water and bought some stores. Our aim was to leave at High Water Dover – using the ebb to help us get round *Cap Gris Nez,* where the streams run up to three knots on springs.

So, at 17.30 we started the engine and motored out, hoisting sail as *Oregon* cleared the harbour. Finding an offshore southeasterly breeze, we turned round the Cap at 23.30, and headed for the harbour entrance at *Boulogne Sur Mer,* arriving in the yacht harbour at 01.40. It seemed like progress After a good night's sleep, the crew hit the shops – and I acquired my first Swiss army knife, for about five bob, plus stacks of good fishing hooks.

Once again, we left under engine, found very light airs, and had to tack often – heading in a southerly direction. After a long spell, it seemed better to close up to the shore and drop anchor before the flood tide started. We found a great spot a few miles east of Dieppe, near a stony beach suitable for the dinghy, and anchored in five fathoms. This turned out to be *Berneval,* where the commandos blew up a German Radar Station before the big Canadian raid at Dieppe.

When ashore, we found a large memorial to the commandos. A path through a gap in the cliffs led us to an *Estaminet,* and a fantastic meal. Walking back in the dark, it wasn't difficult to imagine the bold Commandos landing in the same spot as we had (surrounded by 300-feet-high cliffs.) and going on to blow their target.

Our tidal strategy worked out as long as the winds remained light and variable, and we repeated it when there wasn't enough wind to beat the tide.

Progress improved, and soon the *Le Havre* Lights loomed over the cliffs at *Cap D'Antifer.* Once round this massive headland, the main lighthouse at *Cap de la Hève* appeared, with a lightship at the buoyed channel into our destination. The wind died, so we switched on the engine and motored in – as dawn broke on Thursday 10th August.

Jack Noble and my brother George nipped ashore to collect mail. After lunch, we crossed the *Seine* to *Trouville,* where the yacht harbour had more facilities. Here we got stuck awaiting Jack's cheque – he was due a final payment from Uncle Sam's "GI Bill of Rights", and couldn't afford to miss it. So we worked on the boat and made friends with young locals – keen to show us where the *vin* was good.

Oregon & Crew

Brother George had to get the cross-channel ferry on Saturday, and be back in Dundee to start work on Monday. We travelled with him to make sure he got away okay.

The days passed pleasantly, with swimming on the beach at *Trouville*, and being entertained by the voices of budding Edith Piafs in the local bistros. Many visitors came aboard, keen to hear our plans, and they invited us to eat at their homes. The skipper managed to fall in love with *Chantal*, a stunningly beautiful young French woman.

I began to worry we would never leave *La Belle France*.

Anyway, we signed up a replacement crewman – Dominique – who wanted to get to *Belle Isle* in the Bay of Biscay, and was happy to contribute to our costs. At last... we got under way again, and sailed out on the 22nd August, bound for *Cherbourgh*.

When crossing the Bay of Seine, almost out of sight of land, we didn't know our heading took us past the Normandy Beaches. Owing to fluky winds and strong tide, we anchored of *Barfleur*, and saw many fishing boats heading out. This prompted us to motor in and buy bread. We waited three hours – the tradition was to bake a week's supply, roasted in the round, and kept for a week. It seemed to take forever.

Next stop *Cherbourgh*, where a visiting Argentinian battleship lay at anchor. They had "Liberty" boats taking crew ashore, so we followed and found a yacht basin. The love-struck Jack caught a late train back to *Trouville*, intent on proposing to *Chantal!*.

When he returned the following day, he had the cheque but no *fiancé*, so we now planned our departure. Dominique decided it was taking too long to get to *Belle Isle*, so he jumped ship and left us on our own again. Whether we celebrated too well or departed in a hurry doesn't really matter. But we left after a farewell party with two chaps from the yacht we had tied up against.

These lads, who came from the Solent to buy wine, never sailed at night. They planned on leaving at dawn and dashing across *La Manche* at top speed – to arrive in the Solent before sunset! We should have done the same. Leaving at 20.00, meant running into the worst conditions of the voyage so far. As soon as clearing the west breakwater, we set the sails and cut the engine.

I was heading to pass about five miles off the Big Light at *Cap de La Hague,* and in response to the gusty south wind, we had the wisdom to put three reefs in the main and two in the stay sail. Jack turned in, leaving me on a westward heading to clear Alderney and the *Casquets.*

Shortly after passing the *Cap* we found ourselves caught by the dreaded "Race of Alderney". Even when I headed north, running before a fresh breeze, we still moved south. My mistake was not calling Jack – because I couldn't leave the deck. Conditions proved awful – the jib blew into many pieces, waves kept breaking aboard, and I couldn't access the chart. It seemed to me the race must carry us towards the dreaded *Minquiers* – a vast area of rocks and reefs!

Anyway, *Oregon* made ground bit by bit. But daybreak saw us flung out as the race turned and the sea subsided. Now we were getting somewhere, and by evening, sighted Start Point Lighthouse on the South Coast of England. The shipping forecast told us that a small depression in the western approaches would move north at speed. And the wind would veer from south-west to north-west – great!

With my recently acquired meteorology skills, I reckoned to head south (with nearly forty miles of clear water) and start heading westerly as the wind veered. We went about, and headed south – confident in following the wind around to clear Ushant by at least twenty miles. Many ships crossed ahead of us. As *Oregon* followed the veering wind, progress improved, and we burst into the Bay of Biscay, heading for Spain.

We rounded the tip of *Finnisterre* by keeping twenty miles off the Outer Islands, with its major lighthouse, *Isle de Quesant,* or Ushant, as we all called it. Several other channels exist inside Ushant, but they are treacherou and studded with rocks. Most British ship owners insisted that mariners always stayed at least twenty miles off. That momentous day when we burst into the Bay of Biscay was the 31st August 1950 – a little late in the year for my liking, and much colder than expected.

The strength of the wind grew, so we set our storm canvas, and noticed a tremendous difference in motion and handling, but little or none in speed. Cooking was a pain, often reduced to hot soup and a bar of chocolate. Our clothes and bedding never dried, and our oilskins stayed on till bedtime. Although we pumped the bilge as dry as possible, the residue kept the cabin decks wet and slippery – and raised a foul smell.

At noon on the 1st September, we found ourselves 101 miles nearer Spain than the previous day. That raised a subdued cheer.

Keeping a good course under these conditions is a formidable task, and we did two-hour watches all night. Two-hour work is fine, but two-hours sleep is a different story – especially when faced with a day's work of cooking, pumping, handling and making sail. So we tried three-hour watches, and they worked better.

The man going off watch would nip below (having lashed the helm) and turn up the hurricane lamp hanging in the galley. Then he lit any Primus stove that sounded like it had some paraffin (kerosene) in it, put a kettle on, and then, and only then, called his relief.

You will no doubt understand this unfortunate wretch's feelings as he lay, wet and stiff, in the lee bunk. The gentle hiss of the Primus stove soothed frayed nerves. The watch on deck always overflowed with grand tales of the speed made, how easy she steered, how mild the night – and yet, always seemed desperate to escape to the relatively warm bunk.

I will never forget the night Jack shouted after me, as I crawled out into the cockpit – "If you want me during the night, hesitate to call me," and disappeared under the blanket with huge chuckles. During those first few days of real open-water, I often found comfort in seeing the many ships that passed – making it impossible to feel lonely.

Slowly but surely, most of the ships faded farther away to westward. On the 2nd August, and by next day, we saw nothing but the smoke of passing vessels we couldn't follow. The wind fell and backed west. Nights left us becalmed, and feeling safe, we lit our hurricane lamp before going to bed.

On the evening of the 4^{th,} we found ourselves about twenty-eight miles northward of Cape Ortegal, and often becalmed. After a council of war, and a quick survey of the Captain's cigarette situation – now hopeless – we made up our minds that, when the wind came, we would head for *La Coruna*.

To pass the time, Jack tried starting our Kelvin engine (Leaping Lena), and found both cylinders full of Biscay water. This was a disadvantage caused by our exhaust-cooling system. It required an over-side plug and someone to put it in. After several hours of swinging, and burning-out of the combustion chambers, we took the magneto from the oven and coaxed Lena to leap. She also conjured up a very wicked offshore wind, as if to warn us of the rather ugly cliffs.

That night will always be a mystery to me; the wind seemed possessed of great strength, and yet we hardly heeled, but did some great bursts of speed. It shifted constantly, in a blackness like the inside of Hell – which prevented us from seeing our pennant, but gave the wake an ethereal glow.

The flash of Cape Prior light soon brought us out of the shadow, and in no time we made in for lofty Hercules Tower.

I had forgotten a line I was towing. It had a two-inch spoon bait, and was in fact the old log line. I had stoppered it to the gallows thread, and made fast to the end of the port topping lift tackle. As Jack went forward to set a larfer jib, I almost felt a *ping* (as the thread broke) and saw the main boom convulse like a living thing. When I pulled in my line, I saw it had carried away at the brass weight – my disgust knew no bounds. I had meant to remove the weight earlier!

Next day, noticing we had passed over a fourteen-fathom bank, I assumed that a Merlo or large Tuna was the culprit.

We dallied in *La Coruna* for a day and a night before pushing on for *Vigo*. The first day was a miserable, wet, windlass drag that took us halfway to *Sisargus Island*. When we took in the mains'l before going to bed, the pale lights winking through the rain (like baleful eyes) and the soughing of the cockpit scuppers, had a depressing effect.

We awoke early to the gentle flaying of our head sails, and found a light north-easterly breeze. This was a northerly extension of the Portuguese trade winds, and it felt wonderful roll southwards again.

At noon, we passed *Cape Villano*, with *Oregon* doing better than six knots. A mighty swell blotted out our horizon for long periods, but at least it was with us. The rushing swoop down the lee-side added to our high spirits. I was mighty pleased with myself when one of my light lines brought in a small Garfish. Jack soon had it in the pan. It had rows of wicked teeth, like its West Indian counterpart, and made a tasty dish.

In *Vigo*, we had an excellent reception at the *Club Nautico*, and spent about a week doing repairs and taking on stores.

We had intended drying *Oregon* out in the local fishing basin, to see if the caulking was still tight, but changed our minds after noting it made no water from day to day. I found out, by chatting in Spanish with an old fisherman, how to make cheap lures for Tuny fish. He assured me his double hooks, dressed in corn silk, would catch many *atuns* before coming unstuck.

The dressing for a double iron hook to catch "Tuny" fish was quite simple and very effective. The hooks available locally had flat spade ends, so the first job was to create an eye. This I did by winding white cotton twine along the body, from where the two hooks separated, to the spade, and then making a small loop beyond the spade. Repeated three or four times, this created a white body with a strong eye. After that, we added corn silk in layers – all tied down with more white cotton.

The corn silk was about three inches long and by adding this from the starting place we soon had a light-weight golden body. To complete the dressing, we cut a strip of red bunting, about two inches long, and hooked on to the hook. The idea was to "trawl" this lure along the surface when sailing at about six knots. The lure would jump from wave top to wave top, in the same way as baby squid do in coastal waters. It proved an efficient catcher of *atun*.

On the 15th September, with everything ready, we slipped out of harbour in the early afternoon, having the ebb to take us down the bay. Our luck was normal, so the sails fell slack in the southern passage, shortly after nightfall.

The running swell made a breeze as each roller flowed past. Our nerves, jarred by the canvas slapping, gear rattling and surf booming on either hand, were far from comforting. When the wind finally arrived, it was southerly, and by next evening blew fresh. The accompanying sea, in opposition to the swell, made life in *Oregon* almost unbearable. Steady rain fell and tended to extinguish our hurricane lamp.

Although all commerce passed us on each side, we both gave up in the small hours of the morning – and fell, exhausted, into our bunks. The noise of bilge water rushing back and forth lulled us to sleep, and we didn't even notice the cold. The spell of bad weather soon passed, thank goodness, and a trade wind blew fresh and fine when we tumbled out on deck next morning. Next stop Maderia – and on our way in no uncertain manner.

Our speed seldom dropped below four knots – the best day's run was 140 miles. Watches became irksome, and if we could miss them every other day without loss of distance, we did so. By this means, we managed to average about 100 miles per day, and felt the benefit of the extra sleep.

A day out of *Vigo*, our first tunny fish came aboard with a great deal of struggling. We caught several fine ones, around the eight-pound size, and immensely enjoyed their fried steaks. After crossing the 100 fathom line, however, we had no more bites – and never caught another tunny fish during the voyage.

On the run to Maderia, the main points of concern became bilge water and bread. The former assumed alarming proportions, and our hand bilge pump, a small Simpson & Lawrence Diaphragm, didn't seem to make any difference. We had done about 100 strokes each after coming off watch, and that almost dried the bilge. At this stage we did 500 strokes each. Our combined total, on several days, amounted to over 3,000. It seemed that the pump failed to lift the proper amount of water, so, until reaching Funchal, we had wet feet at meals.

In our isolated state, the bread shortage loomed large – the shore variety lasted two or three days at the most. I felt very proud of my first attempt at loaf making – self-raising dough placed in a cake tin and baked under an upturned biscuit tin. This proved the best oven arrangement – a small loaf of about one pound took around thirty-five minutes. We soon found that the more salt I used the nicer the bread – so we mixed our dough with pure sea water. To conserve our eighty-four-odd gallons of drinking water, we boiled all our vegetables in the same way – and soup, porridge, etc. we also made with a high percentage. On the ninth day from *Vigo*, we sighted the peaks of *Porto Santo*.

I will not dwell on our stay in *Funchal*, in case you go rushing off there next year. Our plan was to stay for a short spell, getting everything in tip-top condition before the long hop. It had been our original intention to follow the sailing ship route to the West Indies – dropping southwards on a gentle curve, and levelling off due west on the 20th parallel. At the approach to the West Indies, we would slip through the Mona Passage between *Porto Rico* and *Santo Domingo*, and run to Jamaica before the strong south-easterly breezes.

If stores fell short, we could stop in *Puerto Rico* without much fear of trouble. A meeting with another adventurer (a former convoy commander during the Second World War) planted a new seed. He was Admiral Goldsmith, master of the yacht *Diotima*, and bound for Barbados. I took a tracing of his large-scale chart, and told him we might go there if we made poor time. *Funchal* was the only place where officials took our passports, and didn't return them until both of us had boarded and made ready to sail.

Our departure was much the same as our previous ones – quiet and unattended. We ate a hearty meal before weighing anchor and ghosting out into the night – backed by a light off-shore breeze. It wanted an hour off midnight, Saturday the 30th September 1950. Both of us felt a little subdued, and I could not help looking back at the lights of a mail boat anchored in the bay. The night was not as empty as we imagined. A loud, startling hail rang out ahead, and a wildly brandished flare broached the darkness. In the nick of time, we altered course to avoid running down a fisherman in a small boat – he had kept his flare close to the water.

Bill Shoots the Sun

The strong trades that had brought us to Madeira now had a respite, and we contented ourselves with short runs to the south'ard in search of a new wind. Twelve miles a day, most of them by current, is mighty discouraging at the beginning of a 3000 mile passage.

It took five days before "old faithful" filled our sails, and we wasted no time in setting all plain sail. In the calm before the winds came back, we had a close-up of our new companions – the dolphins. These beautiful sea-creatures, described so well by Alain Gerbault as being "electrically coloured", created an impressive picture as they circled the yacht – giving us the once over. They proved to be harbingers of the north-east trade winds that were to take us so far – and we set about our tasks with new zest.

The ripple and splash of our bow wave had a wonderful, psychologically soothing effect when we relaxed in the cabin, and it was possible to judge our speed by the varying sound. Our first joy was brief, as the next day Jack reported the radio battery dead – and that evening the pump broke away from its bracket, and we couldn't secure it anywhere.

Turning back would mean the end of our trip, so we stood on and made light of our troubles. Joy arrived with the discovery that bailing with a saucepan into buckets was much easier than pumping. Once we got the hang of passing a full bucket out the hatch, everything became simple. We did ten buckets each after breakfast, and ten after supper – bilge water never appeared on the deck again. This amounted to about eight gallons a day, and I'm glad to say, it never increased.

All our attempts to make *Oregon* self-steering before the wind proved useless. She either came head-to-wind on one side or the other, or she didn't make any speed at all. Both ways, she chafed sails and gear, so we abandoned the twin headsail plan altogether. After some thought, and a lot of watching, we matched the power of the mains'l against a stays'l sheeted to the tiller.

This was a huge success – variable to meet all kinds of conditions. It will be readily understood that the mains'l in a cutter tends to drive the ship to windward. Keeping the main sheet right out, and the wind fine on the opposite quarter, blankets the stays'l. But as soon as the ship edges round to windward the stays'l fills, leans up on the tiller, and you hold a steady course. Watching the tiller counter every attempt *Oregon* made to veer off was great fun.

We chortled with real glee at the thought of no more watches, and sat up late the first night – like misers counting money. The drawback was our limited choice of courses, but we decided our general direction was good, and changed the gear from time to time.

To save fuel, we burned no lights. After the evening bailing, and before turning in, Jack and I sat on deck and smoked. A wonderful experience, with nothing to detract from the natural beauty and solitude. On moonless nights our wake flowed like green flame, and our sea-sharpened eyes picked out dolphins keeping pace abreast the rudder.

One evening, as I stood in the cockpit shooting the stars, a fair-sized flying fish struck the coach-roof and landed on the side deck with a great rattling of its "wings". On account of our generous freeboard, we never found more than five flying fish and two small squids on deck, which was rather disappointing. I had hoped to pick up enough every morning to make breakfast, but we did catch some Dorado. Fried fillets of this kind of fish are a real treat to the lonely mariner, and in my estimation, well worth the trouble of catching.

The wind continued north-easterly, at about force 4 to 5, until the 16th October when, about halfway to Barbados, it faded away and kept us completely becalmed. Our noon position that day was 17 ° 29´ N, 35° 58´ W – and for five days we drifted slowly westward.

It was miserable at first, with the swell still running and our motion becoming unbearable. The oily sea and blistering sun seemed to mock us – every movable thing added its squeak or rattle. We managed some running repairs when the swell subsided a bit, but our mains'l was getting beyond help. Seven out of twelve reef points in each band were herring-boned in – few seams had escaped. As it was a hand-sewn Egyptian cotton sail, I guessed it was of pre-war vintage – so it wasn't surprising.

On taking stock, I found a fortnight's supply of water – if careful – so we had no choice but to head for Barbados. This was the first time we caught any rain-water. During two heavy down-pours, I filled a four-gallon can and an enamel basin. Next day, we did a large wash and had real baths. Whilst sailing, we took turns of climbing down to the bobstay to enjoy the sea rushing up around our necks – as *Oregon* pitched.

We sighed with relief when a steady south-easterly breeze came up on the 21st October, and once again the sky dappled with small cumulus clouds. Our speed never seemed to reach its old heights though, and we assumed the inch-long barnacles bore the responsibility. The infestation covered our rudder and forefoot, and probably the keel, but we couldn't see it. Growth dated from *Funchal*, because we had inspected her there while swimming. By the time we reached Barbados, those barnacles had become two inches long.

The 31st October, found us 322 miles east of Ragged Point, Barbados, and we hadn't seen a ship. Jack's tobacco was almost finished, and mixing tea leaves with the remnants caused some hilarity among the crew. Our menu became limited, and our staple diet consisted of potatoes, bread, and tinned meat. Fish became fewer, though not in the sea, and I had depleted my tackle. I longed for some real piano wire and stainless hooks, as many fish broke away.

By taking simultaneous sights of stars and the moon, I was able to pinpoint our G.M.T. to the nearest minute, after careful interpolation. That meant confidence in our longitude to within fifteen minutes of arc. Knowing our latitude as we did, and by sailing due west, we felt confident about making a landfall. However, as we reduced the miles, our speed seemed to fall in proportion. The last few days, we sat up late (burning precious paraffin in the Tilley lamp) practising fancy knots and watching the compass from time to time.

I puzzled over why I couldn't see any sharks at our Latitude of 13° N., although it was very hot. The first sign of them came with the loss of a six-inch spoon bait from my heaviest line. I renewed it right away on discovering the loss, and arranged the line in short coils, each with a twine stopper. I also made the bucket lanyard fast to the last coil to act as an alarm. The following day at breakfast, the trap went off, and we spent the next hour trying to kill our first shark.

A noose made in the line and dropped over his head did the trick. We made it fast to the jib halyard block, and swung him clear of the water. He died a quick death. When stretched out, it measured six feet. We took the fins and tail, and the rest (which didn't smell at all appetising) went overboard. After this, it was hopeless trying to catch ordinary fish, as the sharks appeared all around. They damaged or carried away all my remaining gear, so I gave up. By Sunday, 5th November, we often climbed aloft and peered to the west

My luck was in and I sighted land first – at one-o'clock in the afternoon – and we judged it twenty miles due west from our position. Our noon fix had put us twenty-four miles off, and we had done nothing but drift since, so we felt mighty pleased with our navigation. Falling rain blotted our new-found treasure, and no lights penetrated the dark. It was hard to accept we neared the end of this long passage.

Staying up all night enabled us to cover a good distance, aided by rain-squalls. Progress was slow, however, and Monday night found us two miles south of South Point Lighthouse, and becalmed. Tuesday saw several sails to seaward, closing rapidly. We soon identified them as fishermen in open boats, using oars as well as sails.

By breakfast, desperation had set in. Our engine refused to start. The drift took us further away from land. We hailed a passing fisherman, managed to get a tow out of the current, and finally dropped anchor in Carabile Bay at 1pm – thirty-seven days out from Madeira.

Jack, so glad to stretch his legs again and visit real shops, decided to give up wandering for good. Perhaps he still carried a torch for the beautiful *Chantal*. He sold *Oregon* to a local yachtsman, before completing his journey home to Texas in comfort.

I was lucky enough to find a ship in need of a second mate, and soon found myself heading back to Scotland. It seemed strange, altering course in any direction without heeding the wind, but I drew no real satisfaction from our method of propulsion. You never see a dolphin from a fast-moving ship – and the flying fish scatter at your approach.

Bill's sketch of a flying fish

Dorado

Glossary

All Plain Sail:- full sail hoisted, no reefs.

Bending on:- to secure sails to their spars, this would be say at the start of the season or when replacing a sail with a new one.

Chart:- is the graphic representation of the maritime area and adjacent coastal regions.

Clew:- the aft (rear) corner of a sail, where the sheets are attached on all foresails.

Fathom:- a measurement of 6 feet, all charts were originally published showing depths in fathoms until metrication.

Fix:- chart position derived by 2 or 3 hand compass bearings of conspicuous landmarks or radio beacon signals plotted on the chart. The intersecting bearings are also known as a " cocked hat". This method of coastal navigation was used before the availability of Decca or GPS (global positioning system) in use today.

Genoa:- a foresail that overlaps the mainsail when set, originally known as an overlapping jib. Often referred to as the *Genny*.

Gybe:- turning the stern of a sailing vessel through the wind when on a downwind course. This change of course results in the sails changing their set to the opposite side and should be controlled by adjusting the main and Genoa sheets through the turn.

Handing the sails:- the process of lowering and stowing away the sails.

Iron topsail:- sailors slang for using the engine for propulsion (the topsail would only be hoisted on the original tall ships to maintain speed in light winds.

Jib:- foresail which does not overlap the mast or mainsail when set.

Knot:- measurement of speed at sea, 1 nautical mile (NM) is 6,076 feet and is defined as one minute of latitude (the North / South Meridian lines drawn horizontally on all charts).

Lee:- the sheltered side of any feature or away from the wind. Often described as *in the lee*. The leeward side of a vessel is downwind, the windward side is upwind where the vessel is the reference point.

Luff:- the leading edge of any sail.

Points of sailing:- Beating or tacking, sailing upwind at the closest possible wind angle (40 - 50 degrees apparent). Reaching is sailing across the wind and can be *close, beam* or *broad reaching* with beam representing 90 degrees apparent wind. Running is sailing downwind at 180 degrees apparent wind.

Port:- the left hand side of the vessel when viewed facing forward.

Reef:- the process of reducing sail area due to strengthening winds. Although foresails can be reefed by a roller furling mechanism they are often replaced with a smaller sail (no.1,2,3 and storm jib).

Sheet:- the rope or line used to control and trim (optimise the set) the sail as in jib sheet or mainstream.

Starboard:- the right hand side of the vessel when viewed facing forward.

Tack:- the sailing manoeuvre which turns the bow of the vessel through the wind and setting the sails on the new heading. Port tack is when the sails are set to a wind direction from the port side. Starboard tack is when they are set to a wind direction from the starboard side. Tack also refers to the forward lower corner of a sail where it is secured to the vessel or her masts.

12728830R00083

Printed in Poland
by Amazon Fulfillment
Poland Sp. z o.o., Wrocław